YOUR KNOWLEDGE HA

- We will publish your bachelor's and master's thesis, essays and papers

- Your own eBook and book - sold worldwide in all relevant shops

- Earn money with each sale

Upload your text at www.GRIN.com and publish for free

Bibliographic information published by the German National Library:

The German National Library lists this publication in the National Bibliography; detailed bibliographic data are available on the Internet at http://dnb.dnb.de .

Imprint:

Copyright © 2016 GRIN Verlag, Open Publishing GmbH
Print and binding: Books on Demand GmbH, Norderstedt Germany
ISBN: 9783668412217

This book at GRIN:

http://www.grin.com/en/e-book/354941/the-role-of-emotions-in-effective-negotiations

Niklas Lochner

The Role of Emotions in Effective Negotiations

GRIN Publishing

GRIN - Your knowledge has value

Since its foundation in 1998, GRIN has specialized in publishing academic texts by students, college teachers and other academics as e-book and printed book. The website www.grin.com is an ideal platform for presenting term papers, final papers, scientific essays, dissertations and specialist books.

Visit us on the internet:

http://www.grin.com/

http://www.facebook.com/grincom

http://www.twitter.com/grin_com

The Role of Emotions in Effective Negotiations

Bachelor Thesis by

Niklas Lochner

December 22, 2016

Table of Contents

TABLE OF FIGURES   VIII

ABBREVIATIONS   IX

1 INTRODUCTION   1

   1.1 Aim and Structure of the paper   1

2 INTRODUCTION TO NEGOTIATIONS   3

   2.1 Conflicts – The Cause of Negotiations   3

   2.2 Definition of Negotiation   4

   2.3 Distributive and Integrative Negotiations   5

   2.4 Types of Negotiators   5

      2.4.1 Hard Bargainers   5

      2.4.2 Soft Bargainers   6

      2.4.3 Principled Bargainers – The Harvard Concept   6

3 EMOTIONS   8

   3.1 The Challenge of Defining Emotions   8

   3.2 The Origin of Emotions   9

      3.2.1 The Appraisal Theory   9

      3.2.2 Limbic System - The Neuroscience of the Appraisal Theory   10

3.3 Functions of Emotions   11

   3.3.1 Motivation   11

   3.3.2 Communication   11

   3.3.3 Decision Making   12

4 PERCEIVING EMOTIONS   14

   4.1 The Concept of Emotional Intelligence   14

   4.2 Recognition of Emotions Through Non-Verbal
   Communication   16

      4.2.1 The Six Basic Emotions   16

      4.2.2 Macro Expressions   17

         4.2.2.1 Surprise   18

         4.2.2.2 Fear   21

         4.2.2.3 Happiness and Enjoyment   23

         4.2.2.4 Disgust   25

         4.2.2.5 Sadness   26

         4.2.2.6 Anger   28

      4.2.3 Subtle Expressions   30

      4.2.4 Micro Expressions   31

5 UNDERSTANDING EMOTIONS IN THE CONTEXT OF A
NEGOTIATION   33

   5.1 Deception and Lies   33

      5.1.1 Masking Deceit   34

      5.1.2 The Three Meta-Emotions of a Lie   35

         5.1.2.1 Detection Apprehension   35

5.1.2.2 Deception Guilt   36

5.1.2.3 Duping Delight   38

5.2 Different Personalities Require Different Negotiation Approaches   39

5.2.1 The Big Five Personality Traits   39

5.2.2 Machiavellianism   41

5.2.3 The Influence of Personality on the Negotiation Strategy   42

6 STRATEGIC USE OF EMOTIONS IN NEGOTIATIONS   45

6.1 The Difference Between Positive and Negative Emotions   45

6.2 The Classification of Emotional Negotiation Strategies and Tactics   46

6.2.1 Strategies to Diminish Negative and Stimulate Positive Emotions   47

6.2.1.1 Emotional Negotiation Preparation   47

6.2.1.2 Mirroring   48

6.2.1.3 Showing Tactical Empathy   49

6.2.1.4 Taking a Break   50

6.2.1.5 Changing the Players or the Place   50

7 CONCLUSION   52

8 REFERENCES   53

APPENDIX   60

Table of Figures

Figure 1: Appraisal Theory (Schmitz-Atzert *et al.* 2014, p. 136)...................................9
Figure 2: Neutral Facial Expression (Eilert 2013, p. 97)...18
Figure 3: Signs of Surprise (Eilert 2013, p. 69)...20
Figure 4: Signs of Fear (Eilert 2013, p. 67)..22
Figure 5: Signs of Happiness – Social vs. Duchenne Smile (Eilert 2013, p. 79).........24
Figure 6: Signs of Disgust (Eilert 2013, p. 73)...26
Figure 7: Signs of Sadness (Eilert 2013, p. 77)...28
Figure 8: Signs of Anger (Eilert 2013, p. 71)..30
Figure 9: Decision Matrix for the Selection of Negotiation Strategies and Tactics 43
Figure 10: Classification Model for Emotional Negotiation Strategies and Tactics......47
Figure 11: The Zygomaticus Major (2014b, http://bit.ly/2hfeT1E) 61
Figure 11: The Orbicularis Oculi (2014a, http://bit.ly/2hoYPZg) 62

Abbreviations

AG	Aktiengesellschaft (joint-stock company)
bn	Billion
e.g.	For example
et al.	Et alii – "and others"
etc.	Et cetera – "and other things"
ibid.	ibidem – "in the same place"
IQ	Intelligence Quotient
MI	Multiple Intelligences
ms	Milliseconds
n.d.	No date
p.	Page
pp.	Pages
s	Seconds
TSA	Transportation Security Administration
vs.	Versus

1 Introduction

Whether people are bargaining for the price for a flower at the florist around the corner, a teenager negotiating about the time he has to be home at night or the German Bayer AG negotiating a $66bn takeover deal with Monsanto[1], negotiations happen every day for different reasons.

Even though we are negotiating every day, there is still a misunderstanding about negotiations that often jeopardizes the outcome of the negotiation. Most people think that negotiating is a sequence of rational decision processes but, as a matter of fact, negotiating involves a dimension that is most often underestimated or ignored: emotions. These might be positive emotions like happiness or negative emotions like disappointment and guilt, but what they all have in common is that they significantly impact negotiations.

This lack of awareness about the influence of emotions on negotiations often leads to negotiation strategies that ignore emotions, even though, recognizing and using emotions can significantly improve the negotiation experience and results.

Based on the assumption that emotions do influence negotiations, this thesis focuses on the question, how different emotions influence the negotiation and which skills and knowledge are necessary in order to improve negotiations through emotional intelligence.

1.1 Aim and Structure of the paper

As mentioned, the central task of the bachelor thesis "The Role of Emotions in Effective Negotiations" is to examine the influence of emotions on negotiations and how emotions can be used to increase their overall efficiency.

This bachelor thesis is divided into seven chapters. Following the introduction with the structure and aim of the paper, chapter 2 introduces the most important characteristics and elements of a negotiation, including different types and styles of negotiations.

Chapter 3 focuses on the definition of emotions and provides a theory on the origin of emotions, based on the research of leading emotion psychologists. To underline the importance of emotions in negotiations, the second part of this chapter explains which impact emotions can have on the essential parts of negotiations: motivation, communication and decision making.

The next chapter introduces the concept of emotional intelligence as well as its origins and then focuses on the recognition of emotions through

---

[1] BBC News Online 2016

macro, micro and subtle facial expressions. For this purpose, the individual signs for the six basic emotions proposed by Paul Ekman will be introduced. Besides the facial expressions of each emotion, also triggers and differences in intensity of emotions will be identified and explained.

Chapter 5 then focuses on the impact of emotions on the ability to detect deceit and also the influence of different personality traits on negotiation styles that involve emotions. Based on the definition of the Big Five personality traits and the additional trait of Machiavellianism, a model is introduced that classifies personalities according to their proneness for emotional negotiation techniques.

The following chapter deals with the influence of positive and negative emotions on negotiations and introduces different strategies that can be used during negotiations to diminish negative and stimulate positive emotions. The findings of this chapter are summarized in a model that classifies the different strategies according to two dimensions and helps negotiators to choose from the different strategies.

Last of all, chapter 7 summarizes the results and findings about the interdependence between emotions and negotiations.

2 Introduction to Negotiations

To understand the influence of emotions in negotiations, it is necessary to define the term negotiation and understand the basic principles and characteristics of a negotiation. Therefore, the following chapter will focus on the basic characteristics of negotiations, the different types of negotiations as well as the different types of negotiators.

2.1 Conflicts – The Cause of Negotiations

The precondition for every negotiation is the existence of a conflict because there would be no need for a negotiation if all involved individuals had matching interests. Thus, it is important to define the types and levels of a conflict before discussing the three major styles of negotiating.

A conflict can, in general, be defined *"as an interactive process manifested in incompatibility, disagreement, or dissonance within or between social entities (i.e., individual, group, organization, etc.)."* [2] After reviewing several definitions for conflict, Robert A. Baron summarized that most definitions overlap with respect to the following elements:

1. Conflicts include opposing interests between individuals or groups.

2. The opposing interests must be recognized by all parties for a conflict to exist.

3. Every conflict involves beliefs by every party, that the other party will thwart, or has already thwarted, its interests.

4. A conflict is a process that develops out of existing relationships and past interactions.

5. Actions by one side result in thwarting of the other's goals. [3]

Even though this definition includes most elements of a negotiation, Robert A. Baron suggests a further definition that includes the dimension of emotion. Baron defines a conflict „*as an ongoing process involving not only opposed interests, but also, in at least some instances, negative feelings and negative thoughts about one's adversary.*" [4]

---

[2] Rahim 2001, p. 18

[3] Baron 2013, pp. 198–199

[4] *ibid.*, p. 199

2.2 Definition of Negotiation

In order to resolve a conflict without physical violence, negotiations are an indispensable solution. The co-founder of the famous Harvard Negotiation Project, William Ury, defines a negotiation as *"the process of back-and-forth communication aimed at reaching agreement with others when some of your interests are shared and some are opposed."* [5] As illustrated before in the introduction, negotiations are not limited to formal business negotiations on a controversial dispute, rather it is also the informal activity that an individual or a group engages in order to acquire something from another party.[6]

A summary of researches on negotiation by Lewicki et al. from 1992 identifies six major characteristics that all negotiations share, whether they are formal or informal.

1. A negotiation involves two or more individuals, groups or organizations.

2. Between the parties a conflict exists that focuses on needs and desires.

3. A negotiation is a voluntary process based on the idea of improving the own position.

4. The fundamental principle of the negotiation is a give-and-take process.

5. The negotiation occurs to find a solution for conflicts where there is no common understanding of how to resolve it.

6. Negotiations always involve tangible (e.g. money or quantity) and intangible factors.[7]

The intangible factors mentioned above are the key element this paper will focus on. They can be defined as a psychological motivation (e.g. emotions) of the negotiating parties. How this psychological motivation can affect the process of negotiating will be illustrated in the following chapters, especially in 2.4 about the three major types of negotiators.

---

[5] Ury 2007, p. 4
[6] *ibid.*
[7] Lewicki *et al.* 2015, pp. 7–9

2.3 Distributive and Integrative Negotiations

Before focusing on different types of negotiators, it is necessary to distinguish between the two major types of negotiations first; distributive and integrative negotiations.[8]

Distributive negotiations are often referred to as competitive, win-lose or zero-sum negotiations. In distributive bargaining, the negotiating parties bargain over fixed and limited resources. The interests of both parties are equal, or at least they seem to be, and a conflict is existent where the win of one side results in a loss on the other side. Due to the limited amount of resources and the equality of interests, negotiators only share information when it provides an advantage. Basically, distributive negotiations are a competition where only one side wins.[9]

In contrast, **integrative negotiations** are more cooperative and focus on finding win-win agreements. The key element of integrative negotiations is a free flow of information that enables the negotiating parties to identify interests. Based on similarities and differences amongst the individual interests, the disputants can identify, develop and select alternatives that satisfy both parties. Due to the exchange of information, integrative negotiations often result in increasing the size of the initial "pie" rather than distributing it.[10]

Negotiations can either be integrative or distributive and in terms of efficiency and fairness, the negotiators who are involved have a major impact on the type of negotiation. How different types of negotiators influence the type of negotiation is therefore illustrated in the following chapters.

2.4 Types of Negotiators

The classic research on negotiation by Fisher, Patton and Ury, as part of the Harvard Negotiation Project, distinguishes between three major types of negotiation styles.[11] This chapter focuses on the basic definition of the hard, soft and principled negotiation style and introduces how emotions can affect a negotiation.

2.4.1 Hard Bargainers

The first negotiator type is the hard bargainer. In general, people associate the hard bargainer with the stereotype of a person who never gives in on his position and takes the lead in distributive negotiations. He sees every negotiation as a rivalry in which the negotiator who insist on the more extreme claims and has more patience will be in the more powerful

---

[8] Walton and MacKersie 1991, 1 ff.

[9] Lewicki *et al.* 2015, pp. 35–37

[10] *ibid.*, pp. 77–78

[11] Fisher and Ury 2011, p. 26

position.[12] This unswayable desire to win can result in a mirroring effect where the opposing party is reacting with a similar competitive behavior.

A simple example for the concept of hard bargaining can already be observed amongst children. Imagine the situation of a mother who is doing her grocery shopping for the week with her 4-year-old son. At the end of the initial shopping, the child insists on getting a package of candy which is refused by the mother. Explaining rationally that there is still candy at home and no need for another package, the mother thinks that she can convince the child to not insist on its claims. Nevertheless the child starts to cry and riot at the cash desk in order to get his candy.

A rational approach will not always convince a hard bargainer to step back from his claims. Unless one party gives in, such competitive behavior often results in distributive negotiations where both parties exhaust their resources, harm their interpersonal relationship and yet often fail to find a common agreement.[13]

2.4.2 Soft Bargainers

The opposite to the hard bargainer is the soft bargainer. Soft negotiators are less interested in insisting on their own position rather than avoiding personal conflicts with the opposing party. In order to achieve amiable settlements, the soft bargainer makes concessions and does not insist on his initial position.[14]

Especially when it comes to negotiations between soft and hard bargainers, the negotiation often ends in a distributive win-lose situation. These agreements can trigger emotional responses like anger, fear or disgust towards the other negotiator that can jeopardize or even harm the personal and professional relationship.

Projected on the example of the mother and her child at the grocery store, the mother will probably follow the soft bargaining approach and give in sooner or later in order to find an agreement and prevent serious harm of the relationship.

2.4.3 Principled Bargainers – The Harvard Concept

With the establishment of the Harvard Negotiation Project in 1983, Roger Fisher and William Ury introduced an alternative way of negotiating.

The principled or interest-based negotiation approach is neither a hard nor soft approach. Instead, it is a combination that is hard on the merits but soft on the people. By separating the problem from the people, the principled negotiation focuses on reaching superior agreements and resolving interest-based conflicts without letting emotions jeopardize the

---

[12] ibid.

[13] ibid.

[14] ibid.

relationship.[15] While this sounds like a completely rational process, the principled negotiation strategy does not ignore the impact of emotional behavior. In fact, it emphasizes to follow four simple steps in a negotiation:

1. Separate the people from the problem.

2. Focus on interests, not positions.

3. Invent options for mutual gain.

4. Insist on using objective criteria.[16]

As mentioned before, separating people from the actual core conflict does not imply to ignore human emotions overall. With this step, the Harvard Principle clearly acknowledges emotions not as a threat but as an intangible factor that can influence a negotiation and should be considered.

Negotiators are not dealing with abstract representatives but with human beings who are disposed to emotional reactions that can either be helpful or destructive, depending on the way the negotiator chooses to deal with them.[17] Thus, paying attention to emotions and knowing how to handle them are major skills of all excelling negotiators.

[15] ibid.
[16] ibid., p. 17
[17] ibid., p. 21

3 Emotions

This chapter focuses on the description of the most important terms and theories regarding emotions and their functions. As of today, there is no universal theory about the nature of emotions which leads to different theories amongst researchers. Therefore, one of the most acknowledged theories is introduced briefly and a widely accepted definition of the term emotion is provided.

3.1 The Challenge of Defining Emotions

We all experience, recognize and show emotions every day but when asked, most people do not have a clear definition for the term emotion. As the psychologists Russel and Fehr noted in their article "Concept of emotion viewed from a prototype perspective",

> *"everyone knows what an emotion is, until asked to give a definition. Then, it seems, no one knows."* [18]

Due to the challenge of defining emotions, different experts have developed several theories and definitions throughout the 20th century. A definition that summarizes the most important aspects of emotions in form of a component theory and is widely acknowledged has been developed by the psychologist Klaus R. Scherer.

Scherer states that an emotion is the temporary synchronization between the most important human sub-systems that initiate the five components of an emotion: cognitive appraisal, physiological regulation, motivation, motor expression and monitoring. Together, those five components are the response to the subjective evaluation of an internal or external stimulus that is significant to the needs and wants of the individual. [19]

A missing part in Scherer's definition is the distinction between moods and emotions. Even though the two terms are often used interchangeably, they differ in several characteristics. First, moods can last for hours or even days while emotions are limited to a few seconds. Second, emotions are always directed towards a specific object or person while moods do not have a specific source and third, emotions are far more intense than moods. [20]

[18] Fehr and Russell 1984, p. 464
[19] Scherer *et al.* 1990a, p. 6
[20] Zimbardo *et al.* 2008, p. 454

3.2 The Origin of Emotions

The research on the origin of emotions is diverse and complex. Therefore it is impossible to strive for completeness in describing the theory on emotions. As of today, the research on emotion is constantly evolving but there are a few theories that had and still have significant impact on it. The working theory for this paper will be a neuroscientific and cognitive approach that has been chosen due to its importance and impact in the recent history of emotional research.[21]

3.2.1 The Appraisal Theory

The basic assumption of the appraisal theory, also known as cognition theory, is that an emotion and its intensity depend on how a person appraises a situation (person, object etc.).[22] For example, a lion can trigger different emotions with different intensities, depending on previous experiences and the individual appraisal of the current situation. While a lion in the wilderness might be appraised as a potential danger that leads to fear, a lion in a zoo is not evaluated as a threat.

The most important representatives of the appraisal theory are Richard Lazarus and Magda B. Arnold. Lazarus states that emotions occur because people understand up to a certain level, that the outcome of a conflict or confrontation with another person or stimulus can involve either harm or benefit. In this context, he defines appraisal as the evaluation of a situation through the knowledge that a person has acquired through individual experiences. Therefore, each emotion is the result of a subjective appraisal process that evaluates the specific harm or benefit that has been or will be evoked.[23]

The whole appraisal theory after Lazarus can be illustrated as follows:

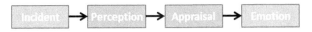

Figure 1: Appraisal Theory (Schmitz-Atzert *et al.* 2014, p. 136)

Once an incident occurs, it is perceived by the person that is directly affected. In a cognitive process, the person evaluates the impact of the situation on his or her current situation with regards to personal goals and motives. This appraisal process then triggers a specific emotion to initiate a response to the incident.

---

[21] Schiewer 2014, p. 29

[22] Brandstätter *et al.* 2009, p. 435

[23] Richard Lazarus 1994, p. 366

To understand how the process of appraisal works within the human organism, the next part will illustrate the involved neuroscientific processes.

3.2.2 Limbic System - The Neuroscience of the Appraisal Theory

From a neuroscientific view, the essential part of the appraisal process takes place in the limbic system. The limbic system is a collective term for brain structures that are substantial for emotion processing. The most important parts of the limbic system are the amygdala, the hippocampus, the cingulate cortex, the hypothalamus and parts of the neocortex, especially the orbitofrontal cortex.[24]

The central part of the limbic system is the amygdala. Each person has two amygdalae, one on each side of the brain. Research has shown that the amygdala performs a major role in processing emotional reactions, modulating memories and influencing the decision-making.[25]

Every information, external or internal stimulus or retrieved experience from the neocortex is evaluated by the amygdala with regards to the possible influence. The evaluation itself is based on previous experiences that had an impact on the person. Depending on the emotion that the amygdala linked to this experience in the past, the evaluation of the current stimulus is significantly influenced by this knowledge.[26]

Based on the appraisal through the amygdala, the hypothalamus releases chemical messengers, e.g. dopamine, and in combination with electrical signals that stimulate the nervous system, we experience a specific emotion that prepares us for a physiological reaction.[27]

In combination with the hippocampus and the neocortex, the amygdala has another important function, the modulation of memories. The amygdala evaluates every stimulus and depending on its importance, the hippocampus links somatic markers to all information (e.g. dopamine or serotonin). This information and the according markers are then stored by the hippocampus in the neocortex and function as the above mentioned knowledge for future evaluations.[28]

From now on, the limbic system is conditioned to this stimulus, person or situation through emotionally marked memories and the limbic system can access the preceding information. Once activated, the somatic markers trigger a diminished version of the emotion that we experienced when the information was stored. The emotional memory is then used to evaluate a situation and make a decision based on previous experiences.[29]

---

[24] Häusel 2014b, p. 50

[25] Roth 2009, 276 ff.

[26] Häusel 2014b, p. 51

[27] *ibid.*, p. 52

[28] *ibid.*, p. 54

[29] *ibid.*

This conditioning of the brain through somatic markers is especially important in social interactions and decision making as the next chapter further illustrates.

3.3 Functions of Emotions

Now that we have established what emotions are and where their origin is, we need to understand their functions. There are many different functions of emotions but the most important ones that are related to negotiations are motivation, communication and decision making.

3.3.1 Motivation

The first important function of emotions is motivation and the resulting behavior. The question is: Why are some people outperforming others in different areas of life?

People might be talented or lucky but Gary Player, a famous golfer, gave the answer: "The harder I practice, the luckier I get."[30] So people are not better than others because of luck or talent, their performance is based on the motivation of improving their current situation.

Everyone has specific goals they want to reach and in this context, emotions encourage us to act in a way that is leading to this goal. They give us a direction to guide us and the motivation to stay focused in order to achieve our goals.[31]

Once you have experienced anger or frustration due to a lost game or negotiation, it is the human nature to strive for better results in the future. Seeking for positive emotions is not just a behavior to feel better, it is an essential feature of human beings. We need motivation through emotion in order to improve our personal life situation and refrain from negative situations that deteriorate the status of our life situation.[32]

In conclusion, emotions are the key to human motivation. They prevent us from harming ourselves and encourage us to seek for life improvements. Increasing the experience of positive emotions and minimizing the experience with negative emotions are major motives of human motivation.[33]

3.3.2 Communication

Emotions are an essential factor that enables people to function within their social environment. Through expressive characteristics like language, facial expressions and body-language, people communicate their emotions to show how they feel and what they think.

[30] Gary Player n.d.
[31] Zimbardo *et al.* 2008, pp. 463–464
[32] Scherer *et al.* 1990b, pp. 42–45
[33] Ekman 2007, xxi

Robert Levenson identified two main functions of emotions in communication. First, expressed emotions allow other people to understand how we feel, and second, they have a direct impact on the other person's behavior.[34]

For example, a person who expresses fear can cause others to become fearful as well which can lead to mass panics. On the other side, a smile that expresses positive emotions can help others to calm down and defuse dangerous and fearful situations.[35] In terms of a negotiation, showing emotions can help to emphasize whether or not we appreciate our negotiation partner and the proposed offer.

So by expressing our emotions, we help others to understand how we feel and what we think, while the ability of perceiving emotions helps us to do the same and function within our social environment.

3.3.3 Decision Making

Making decisions is a major part of the everyday life. People make decisions in the morning if they should get up or not, they decide whether to walk or drive or where to have dinner. It seems like those decisions are purely rational because people evaluate which option is better for reaching their goals.

This view of a person who is only deciding based on a cost-benefit evaluation is called homo economicus, a theoretical model that is no longer applicable today.[36] Especially the psychologist Antonio Damasio significantly changed the view on the process of how people make their decisions. He demonstrates through his experiments, that emotions play a major role in the process of making decisions by analyzing how people with brain damage of the limbic system make decisions.

When Damasio's book "Descartes' Error: Emotion, Reason and the Human Brain" was first published, Damasio and his colleagues had studied 12 patients with a prefrontal brain damage which had an impact on the ability of making decisions and experiencing emotions.[37]

Through various tests with his patients, Damasio was able to proof that emotions have a significant impact on how we make decisions. One of his brain damaged patients once said after a session of presenting several rationally eligible options for action: "And after all this, I still wouldn't know what to do!" [38]

Due to their brain damage, the patients were no longer able to assign an emotional evaluation to different options like normal people would do. As a consequence, the only differentiation they could make between dif-

---

[34] Levenson 1994, pp. 124–125
[35] Ekman 1994, pp. 124–125
[36] Häusel 2014a, p. 116
[37] Damasio 1995, 53 f.
[38] *ibid.*, p. 49

ferent options was rational. The challenge with this kind of decision making is perfectly illustrated by the quote above. Even though all options are valid, the missing emotional evaluation prevents the patient from making a final decision because he is not able to differentiate if the action would be harmful or beneficial for his personal goals.[39]

Damasio's research shows that every decision we make is influenced by emotions. They enable us to make faster and better decisions based on whether or not they are beneficial for our well-being. In consequence, this means that rationality itself always requires emotional input to work properly and therefore emotions need to be considered during negotiations as well.

---

[39] *ibid.*, pp. 34–83

4 Perceiving Emotions

4.1 The Concept of Emotional Intelligence

The concept of emotional intelligence as we know it today is a rather new idea that contradicts the "old" view of intelligence that was defined through the Intelligent Quotient. The term "Emotional Intelligence" is based on the theory of multiple intelligences.

The concept of multiple intelligences was developed by the psychologist Dr. Howard Gardner, professor at the Harvard School of Education, in the late1970's and early 1980's. His book "Frames of Mind: The Theory of Multiple Intelligences" revolutionized the understanding of intelligence as it breaks with the traditional view on intelligence. He suggests that the traditional interpretation of intelligence (IQ) is far too limited and does not reflect the full range of intelligence. Instead, Gardener proposes eight different types of intelligence: linguistic, logical-mathematical, spatial, musical, naturalist, bodily-kinesthetic, interpersonal and intrapersonal intelligence. [40]

The last two types of intelligences build the foundation of what Gardener calls personal intelligence. He defines the two dimensions of personal intelligence as follows:

> "The core capacity [of intrapersonal intelligence] [...] is access to one's own feeling life—one's range of affects or emotions: the capacity instantly to effect discriminations among these feelings and, eventually, to label them, to enmesh them in symbolic codes, to draw upon them as a means of understanding and guiding one's behavior. [...] At its most advanced level, intrapersonal knowledge allows one to detect and to symbolize complex and highly differentiated sets of feelings."

> "The core capacity [of interpersonal intelligence] [...] is the ability to notice and make distinctions among other individuals and, in particular, among their moods, temperaments, motivations, and intentions. [...] In an advanced form, interpersonal knowledge permits a skilled adult to read the intentions and desires—even when these have been hidden—of many other individuals and, potentially, to act upon this knowledge—for example, by influencing a group of disparate individuals to behave along desired lines." [41]

---

[40] Gardner 2011, pp. 1–412
[41] *ibid.*, p. 253

Based on the theory of personal intelligence, Salovey and Mayer *"define emotional intelligence as the ability to perceive and express emotion, assimilate emotion in thought, understand and reason with emotion, and regulate emotion in self and others."* [42]

The term Emotional Intelligence itself popularized through the publication of Daniel Goleman's book "Emotional Intelligence", in 1995. Based on Salovey's and Mayer's definition of emotional intelligence, Goleman further distinguishes between five core areas of emotional intelligence:

1. Self-awareness: The ability to recognize and understand emotions when they occur is the foundation of emotional intelligence. Monitoring and recognizing personal emotions enables us to stay in charge and maintain a clear view on decisions and emotional responses.

2. Self-regulation: Based on the self-awareness, the control over personal emotions ensures that we can regulate our emotions in order to diminish negative and maximize positive emotions.

3. Motivation: Using emotions to motivate ourselves, increase creativity and maintain a focus on important tasks to be more efficient and productive.

4. Empathy: The ability of understanding another person's emotions. In the context of emotional intelligence, empathy can be defined as the key to interpersonal relations.

5. Social Skills: Interpersonal relationships require the skill of identifying emotions of others and handling them in a way to establish rapport and build personal relationships. [43]

These five core areas of emotional intelligence summarize the basic skills that emotional intelligent people share. Gardener, Salovey, Mayer and Goleman significantly changed the view of how intelligence is defined and demonstrated that overall intelligence consists of more than just mathematical or logical intelligence.

---

[42] Sternberg 2000, p. 396
[43] Salovey and Mayer 1990, 191 ff.

4.2 Recognition of Emotions Through Non-Verbal Communication

As shown before, emotions are an important factor for interactions be-tween people. They help us to communicate, make decisions and moti-vate ourselves. Especially in terms of communication, we have different ways to express emotions. No one has to say if he is sad or happy be-cause we all have the innate ability to perceive emotions in others.

Nevertheless, perceiving emotions remains to be difficult for most peo-ple due to the fact that most people do not pay enough attention to the signs of emotions. In order to raise the awareness for the individual signs of different emotions, the following chapter will focus on the expressive signs of the basic emotions and the differences between macro, micro and subtle expressions.

4.2.1 The Six Basic Emotions

In 1872, Charles Darwin published his book "The Expression of the Emo-tions in Man and Animals". Darwin stated that emotions are not culturally learned but innate, which lead him to the conclusion that some emotional facial expressions had to be universal and part of the evolutionary inher-itance.[44]

This idea of emotional facial expressions being universal and devel-oped through evolution was not shared amongst the majority of leading anthropologists of the 20th century.[45] Against the prevalent opinion, Silvan Tomkins published two books about emotions focusing on the same theo-ry as Darwin but due to a lack of evidence, he could not back up his claims. Around this time, in the 1960s, Paul Ekman started his research on facial expressions as part of the Advanced Research Projects Agency of the Department of Defense. In the beginning he wanted to proof Darwin and Tomkins wrong but his research led him to the same conclusion: Some emotions were developed through the natural process of evolution and therefore, different characteristics of emotion expression had to be universal.[46]

In his research, Paul Ekman discovered that the human face is able to show more than ten thousand different expressions but that there are six basic emotions of which the facial expressions are universal and can be recognized by people all over the world, while the expression of other emotions can differ across cultures.[47] The basic emotions Ekman identi-fied are anger, disgust, fear, happiness, sadness and surprise.[48] Important

---

[44] Darwin 1872 **qtd. in** Zimbardo *et al.* 2008, p. 456
[45] Ekman 2007, p. 3
[46] *ibid.*, pp. 1–3
[47] *ibid.*, p. 14
[48] Paul Ekman 1970, p. 156

to note is that Ekman does not claim that these are the only (universal) emotions but the ones that have scientifically proven universal appearances. For example, trust, shame, satisfaction, embarrassment, interest, excitement, envy, love, etc. are also emotions but do not share all characteristic of a universal appearance.[49]

4.2.2 Macro Expressions

Even though we have the innate ability to differentiate between the six basic emotions (and others), we often fail to recognize them because we do not pay enough attention to the signs.

The facial movements that normally express an emotion are called macro expressions. Macro expressions last between 0.5s to 4s[50] and usually appear when someone does not try to suppress or hide his emotions. Other than micro expressions, macro expressions are controlled by the pyramidal tracts that originate in the motor cortex and are responsible for voluntary movements.[51]

Macro expressions of emotions are expressed in three areas of the face. Every emotion has specific and individual signs in all three areas but the importance of the areas can vary across emotions. The parts of the face that are interesting for facial expressions are divided in the upper face with the brows and the forehead, the eyes with the eyelids and the lower face, including the cheeks, mouth, chin and lips.[52]

Although we can recognize these facial movements, false interpretation and missing knowledge can still mislead us. Thus, the following chapters will identify the major signs of the six basic emotions and clarify common mistakes in interpreting these signs. Therefore, the individual signs will be explained and illustrated with the aid of pictures of the full facial expression. For the purpose of highlighting the individual signs of each emotion, the picture that is provided below can be used for comparison as it shows a neutral facial expression.

---

[49] Schmitz-Atzert *et al.* 2014, p. 33

[50] Scherer and Ekman 2014, 332

[51] Eilert 2013, p. 53

[52] Ekman and Friesen 2003, pp. 28–29

Figure 2: Neutral Facial Expression (Eilert 2013, p. 97)

Before discussing the different individual signs of emotions, it is necessary to note that emotions do not always appear in a pure form and can blend with each other. These simultaneously occurring emotions are called "Blended Emotions".[53] They consists of facial expression features of two different emotions, for example a blend of happiness and fear. These blends of emotions are not discussed any further as their characteristics can be derived from the individual features of the two blending emotions and due to the fact that different emotions often occur in sequences rather than in blends.[54]

4.2.2.1 *Surprise*

The first basic emotion to be discussed in this paper is surprise. Of all basic emotions, surprise is the briefest and only lasts for a few seconds at most. Both, the onset and disappearance of surprise as an emotion are sudden, unless the surprising event is continued by new surprising elements.[55] Otherwise, the duration of surprise is extremely short compared to other emotions. Therefore, the short duration is the most reliable sign for true surprise while a surprise expression that last longer than 1s is most often a faked emotion.[56]

Surprise can be triggered by different events or actions but what they all have in common is their sudden and unexpected appearance. When a surprising event unfolds step by step, it will not be surprising as we can prepare for the event. Therefore, surprise will not appear as an emotion

---

[53] Eilert 2013, p. 131

[54] Ekman 2007, p. 69

[55] Ekman and Friesen 2003, p. 34

[56] Eilert 2013, p. 86

when we expect that the event will happen.[57] Suppose that a salesman from one of your suppliers appears in your office to offer you some of his products. If he offers you known products for a price that is common for this quality on the market, you will not be surprised as you already expected it. Therefore, the offer is not unexpected or surprising for you. But, if the salesman offers you a product with innovative features that no competitor can offer and the price remains the same, it is an unexpected event that will most likely surprise you and increase your interest in further negotiations.

As every emotion that will be discussed in the following chapters, surprise can also appear in different intensities. The variations in intensity range from slight surprise to a startle reaction.[58] While you might be slightly surprised by a grade in an exam that is better than expected, the sound of an explosion will likely cause a startle reaction that is by far more intense than surprise. This difference in intensity is also closely related to the four major types of surprise as the intensity leads to differences in the facial expression. The four major types of surprise are the questioning surprise, the astonished surprise, the dazed surprise and the full surprise.[59]

When experiencing surprise, the **eyebrows** are raised and curved which causes the skin below the eyebrow to be stretched due to the raised eyebrows. Some people also show horizontal wrinkles across the forehead but this sign is ambiguous as it does not appear on every face. Without other signs across the face, not only the wrinkles but also the eyebrows are an ambiguous sign. Appearing alone for a few seconds, the raised eyebrows can be a sign for doubt or questioning rather than surprise. In contrast, when only a quick brow-raise occurs, it is often used as a conversational punctuator or if it is accompanied with a slight movement of the head, it can be greeting emblem.[60]

The second sign of surprise can be observed in the **eyes**. In combination with the eyebrows, they are the most important factor in differentiating between the expression of surprise and fear.[61] During surprise, the eyes are opened wider than usual, uncovering the sclera above the iris.[62] Similar to the eyebrows, the surprise eyes can occur alone and can also be a signal for interest rather than surprise but when accompanied by the surprise brows and the surprise mouth, the meaning is unambiguous.[63]

---

[57] Ekman 2007, p. 149

[58] Ekman and Friesen 2003, pp. 36–37

[59] *ibid.*, p. 43

[60] *ibid.*, pp. 37–39

[61] Ekman 2007, p. 167

[62] The colored circular structure in the eye that controls the size and diameter of the pupil is called iris. The iris is surrounded by a white outer layer, the sclera.

[63] Ekman and Friesen 2003, p. 40

When surprise is shown in the **lower face**, usually the jaw drops open causing the lips and the teeth to be apart but still relaxed and not tense. This jaw dropping is dependent on the intensity of the surprise and the more intense the emotion is, the more likely it is that the mouth is widely open. In combination with the other two signs of surprise in the eyes and eyebrows, this is a clear indicator for surprise, while a sole appearance is more likely to be a sign for speechlessness.[64]

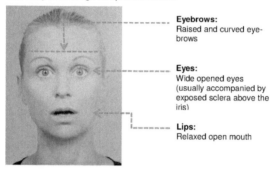

Eyebrows:
Raised and curved eyebrows

Eyes:
Wide opened eyes (usually accompanied by exposed sclera above the iris)

Lips:
Relaxed open mouth

Figure 3: Signs of Surprise (Eilert 2013, p. 69)

As defined, surprise is the briefest of the six basic emotions. The explanation for the short duration is that once the surprising event is evaluated by the limbic system, we move to another emotion. Surprise itself is a neutral emotion that is neither positive nor negative.[65] Depending on the possible impact that the event can have, it is the following emotion that adds a positive or negative impression to the experience. Distasteful surprise yields disgust while surprise about something positive such as a good grade or a new love will turn into happiness. If provocative actions are surprising us, the surprise will lead to anger and a threat which cannot be diminished, we experience fear as a sequel. Surprise is most often followed by fear because most unexpected events are associated with threat and danger.[66]

Due to the close relation between surprise and fear in facial expression and the other reasons mentioned above, fear will be discussed in the following part to highlight the similarities and differences in the expression of fear and surprise.

---

[64] *Ibid.*, pp. 40–42

[65] Eilert 2013, p. 86

[66] Ekman and Friesen 2003, pp. 35–36

4.2.2.2 *Fear*

The emotion that most often follows surprise is fear. It is one of the most important emotions because it enables us to deal with threats by focusing our attention on the source of harm or danger until we can eliminate it.[67] Our survival depends on the ability to learn how to avoid and escape harmful situations and fear is the alarm reaction that gives us the necessary attention and focus to perceive and escape pain and threat.[68]

The emotional trigger of fear is harm. Humans fear the possibility of harm, which has two dimensions: physical and psychological. Psychological harm may include the loss of job, loss of friendship, disappointment or the fear of public speaking. On the other hand, physical harm that can trigger fear includes for example imminent bodily impact. While some triggers of fear are universal, such as the fear when a sudden loss of gravity occurs, other triggers are learned, such as the fear of dangerous animals.[69] Depending on the environment, education and social surroundings, triggers can vary amongst different people, e.g. the fear of insects is much greater in western cultures than it is in eastern countries.

The variations of intensity in fear can reach from anxiety to terror.[70] As mentioned in chapter 3.2.1 about the appraisal theory, events are evaluated according to the impact that they can possibly have on us. Thus, the intensity of fear also depends on the subjective cognitive appraisal of the stimulus. Fear is triggered by threat, which can be further differentiated into immediate and impending threat. Immediate threat usually leads to action that deals with the source of threat by either fighting, fleeing or freezing depending on the preceding appraisal. On the other hand, impending threat leads to increased attention and muscular tension that prepares us to react.[71] During the appraisal of the situation that determines the intensity of fear, the limbic system evaluates the chances of coping with the harm, avoiding it, reducing it or surviving it before it considers the three possible reactions: fight, flight or freeze.[72]

During the experience of fear, the **eyebrows** are drawn together so that the inner corners of the eyebrows appear to be closer than they are in the surprise brow. In addition, the eyebrows are raised and appear much more straightened than they do in surprise. The fear brow is usually, depending on the normal individual facial features, accompanied by horizontal wrinkles across the forehead. In contrast to surprise, these wrinkles do not appear across the entire forehead. If the fear brow appears without

---

[67] Ekman 2007, 155 ff.
[68] Ekman and Friesen 2003, pp. 47–48
[69] Ekman 2007, pp. 152–157
[70] Ekman and Friesen 2003, p. 49
[71] Rhudy and Meagher 2000, 65 ff.
[72] Ekman and Friesen 2003, p. 49

any other signs of fear in the eyes or the mouth, it conveys the message of worry, slight apprehension or restrained fear.[73]

Another sign of fear appears in the **eyes** and in contrast to the other signs of fear in the face, the fear eyes are almost always an unambiguous sign of fear.[74] Similar to the surprise eyes, the fear eyes show a raised upper eyelid which causes the sclera above the iris to be exposed. The difference between surprise and fear in the eyes can be observed in the lower eyelid. While in surprise the lower eyelid is relaxed, it is slightly raised and tensed in fear which may be sufficient to cover parts of the lower iris. As mentioned before, the fear eyes are an unambiguous sign of fear and can appear as a micro expression (see chapter 4.2.4), showing signs of slight or controlled fear through short flashing of the expression.[75]

The last sign of fear can be observed in the **lower face**. In fear, the mouth starts to open and the corners of the lips are drawn back tightly which causes the lips to tense. Standing alone, the fear mouth can have the same meaning as the fear eyes when they appear as a micro expression.[76]

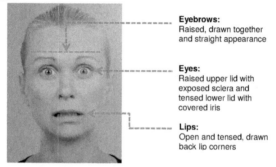

Eyebrows:
Raised, drawn together and straight appearance

Eyes:
Raised upper lid with exposed sclera and tensed lower lid with covered iris

Lips:
Open and tensed, drawn back lip corners

Figure 4: Signs of Fear (Eilert 2013, p. 67)

The previous two emotions, surprise and fear, are closely related in terms of facial expressions. Thus, it is by far more difficult to perceive them as they share some features and only have minor differences. To reliably detect and distinguish between surprise and fear, a lot more attention is required in order to recognize them correctly.

---

[73] *ibid.*, pp. 50–52

[74] Ekman 2007, p. 65

[75] Ekman and Friesen 2003, pp. 52–53

[76] *ibid.*, pp. 53–55

4.2.2.3 *Happiness and Enjoyment*

Happiness is the only emotion, out of the six basic emotions, that is considered a positive emotion. While surprise is neither positive nor negative, all other emotions discussed in this paper are considered to be negative. First of all, we need to distinguish between the four types of happiness; pleasure, excitement, relief and introspectional happiness. Pleasure refers to positive physical sensation such as sexual intercourse, while excitement refers to the psychological sensation of being interested in something that draws your attention and arouses interest.[77] Besides excitement and pleasure, also relief can cause happiness, e.g. when a negative emotion such as fear subsides, we are relieved and often experience happiness as a result.[78] The last type of happiness occurs when something happens that changes the way we see ourselves in a positive manner.[79] For example, if someone is awarded for his research with the Nobel Prize, this person might feel happy about being admired by others.

All four experiences can be defined as triggers for happiness. When you think of situations that caused you to experience happiness, you will probably recognize that happiness often involves more than one of the happiness triggers described above. For example, you might experience excitement while attending a soccer match, pleasure from the physical exertion, self-concept happiness because you're playing well and finally relief because you supported your team and did not let them down.[80] So most of the times, happiness involves more than one trigger and the different types of happiness often blend with each other.

Just like the other basic emotions, happiness does not only vary in the different types, but also in its intensity. It can reach from a mildly happy experience to joy or ecstasy. Furthermore it can be silent or audible, accompanied by a smile, laughter or even tears in its most extreme form. Nevertheless, extreme forms of happiness do not always include laughter or tears as they can be silent as well, only expressed by a subtle smile.[81]

In terms of facial expressions, happiness shares some characteristics with disgust as the appearance of both emotions is primarily visible in the lower face and the lower eyelids.[82] The universal sign for happiness or enjoyable emotions is the smile. We are able to use smiles for different occasions but the most important differentiation has to be made between a real and a false smile. The subtle difference between enjoyment and non-enjoyment smiles is often missed as there is only a slight difference in

---

[77] *ibid.*, pp. 99–100
[78] Ekman 2007, pp. 193–194
[79] Ekman and Friesen 2003, pp. 100–101
[80] *ibid.*, p. 101
[81] *ibid.*
[82] *ibid.*, p. 103

appearance.[83] The first person to discover the difference was the French neurologist Duchenne de Boulogne in 1862, who found that *"The emotion of frank joy is expressed on the face by the combined contraction of the zygomaticus major muscle and the orbicularis oculi."* [84] The zygomaticus major muscle[85] is involved in true as well as in false expressions of happiness or enjoyment through a smile, whereas the orbicularis oculi is only involved in the expression of frank joy because it is nearly impossible to voluntarily contract this muscle. In honor of Duchenne de Boulogne, Paul Ekman later referred to this true expression as the Duchenne smile.[86]

Social Smile:
Raised lip corners,
no involvement of the
orbicularis oculi

Duchenne Smile:
Raised cheeks, wrinkles
under the eyes, crows-feet,
higher visibility of the
naso-labial folds

Figure 5: Signs of Happiness – Social vs. Duchenne Smile (Eilert 2013, p. 79)

In a Duchenne smile, the corners of the lips are slightly raised while drawn back. Depending on the intensity and control over the emotion, this may result in a smile, where the lips stay together, a grin, with the lips parted or even an opened mouth with parted lips and teeth in an intense grin.[87] Furthermore, a rising of the cheeks causes the naso-labial folds to become more apparent. Through the raised cheeks, the lower eyelid is

---

[83] *ibid.*

[84] Duchenne and Cuthbertson 2006, p. 72

[85] See appendix A1 and A2 for further descriptions of the zygomaticus major and the orbicularis oculi

[86] Ekman 2007, pp. 204–207

[87] Ekman and Friesen 2003, p. 103

pushed up and horizontal lines appear below the eye as well as "crow's-feet" at the outer corners of the eyes.[88]

4.2.2.4 *Disgust*

Other than fear, disgust is not concerned with the possible impact, such as harm, of an object, situation or other stimulus. Rather it is focused on the appearance of something and the related aversion. When we are disgusted by something, we are responding with avoidance. Even though the stimulus could be harmless, we don't want to get closer to the source of disgust and try to eliminate it.[89]

While the expression of disgust is universal through different cultures, the triggers of disgust are not. What might be repulsive for people in Germany might be attractive for people in China. The triggers of disgust can be distinguished into different categories but the individual source of disgust might be different from one person to another, as they are learned and not innate.

Disgust is most often triggered by tastes, smells, sights, sounds or touches but even actions, ideas or appearances of people can bring forth disgust.[90] Good examples for different triggers of disgust are table manners. While eating with your hand is a normal behavior in eastern cultures, such as India, western cultures might find it disgusting to eat without cutlery. On the other side, people from India might be disgusted when someone would eat with his left hand, as it is used for unsavory functions such as cleaning your feet.

The previously discussed emotions show signs in at least two facial areas but disgust is primarily visible in the lower face. In disgust, the lower lip is raised and depending on the intensity of disgust and the resulting raise of the upper lip, wrinkles along the sides of the nose appear, better known as nasolabial folds. The lower lip can either be lowered and protruding or raised towards the upper lip. Furthermore, the cheeks are raised and cause the lower eyelid to be pushed up but not tensed. This is especially important as a tensed eyelid would be a sign for anger.[91]

---

[88] *ibid.*

[89] McGinn 2011, pp. 6–7

[90] Ekman and Friesen 2003, pp. 66–67

[91] *ibid.*, pp. 68–71

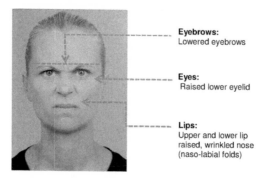

Eyebrows:
Lowered eyebrows

Eyes:
Raised lower eyelid

Lips:
Upper and lower lip
raised, wrinkled nose
(naso-labial folds)

Figure 6: Signs of Disgust (Eilert 2013, p. 73)

4.2.2.5 *Sadness*

Besides anger, fear and disgust, sadness is the fourth negative basic emotion proposed by Paul Ekman. Unlike physical pain that is experienced as distress, sadness is the suffering that occurs due to psychological stimuli like hopelessness, disappointment or loss.[92] Sadness is a form or variation of distress and the main difference that distinguishes them from each other is the way it is expressed. While distress is an active form of suffering that is openly expressed through crying or screaming and where you try to actively remove the source of pain, sadness is defined by passivity. Sadness often occurs when distress is not helpful or signs of sadness are more acceptable in social surroundings so that sadness covers controlled distress.[93] The focus of this chapter will be sadness as the open signs for distress, e.g. crying, are easy to detect while sadness can be more challenging to perceive.

As the definition already points out, sadness is triggered by psychological stimuli such as loss of loved ones, disappointment caused by a promotion or a deal you couldn't get or having no hope to overcome or accomplish something. The message that sadness expresses is based on an evolutional function, it is a call out to other people who recognize the sadness to feel concern and offer comfort.[94]

Important for negotiations is especially the intensity of the emotion, as different intensities provide different messages and differ in the attention needed to perceive them. The intensity of an emotion often results in a different intensity of the corresponding facial expressions as well. The variation of sadness ranges from being sad to extreme experiences of

---

[92] *ibid.*, p. 114
[93] *ibid.*, pp. 114–115
[94] Ekman 2007, pp. 87–89

sadness such as mourning. The facial expressions that come along with sadness can be observed in all three areas of the face.[95]

The strongest and most reliable sign for sadness in the face of others can be observed in the **eyebrows**. The movements of the eyebrows that occur in the presence of sadness are involuntary and the majority of people do not have the ability to deliberately fake this movement. This fact makes the eyebrows the most reliable indicator for sadness as it often leaks the emotion while other parts of the face seem to be neutral.[96] The sadness brow appears when the inner corners of the brows are drawn together and raised so that they have a triangular shape.[97] By drawing together and raising the eyebrows, a vertical wrinkle between the eyebrows appears in most people. If this wrinkle has already been visible before, e.g. due to the age, the wrinkle will likely become deeper and darker.[98] Besides signaling sadness or controlled distress, the eyebrow movements can be used as punctuators for different words or phrases while speaking.[99]

Due to the movements of the eyebrows, the second sign of sadness is automatically initiated in the **eyelids**. The movements in the brows and forehead cause the upper eyelid to slightly drop and cover a higher percentage of the iris. The important point with the upper eyelid dropping is that without the eyebrow movements, it can also be a sign for tiredness or exhaustion instead of sadness.[100] A sign of greater sadness is a combination of the lowered upper eyelid combined with a raised lower eyelid and a glaze that is pointed downward.[101]

Thirdly, sadness can be expressed in the **lower parts of the face** such as the mouth or chin. The sadness mouth can appear in different variations depending on the intensity of the emotion and the control that the person has over it. A slight sadness is expressed through lowered lip corners, while more intense sadness can cause trembling of the lips[102] or a so called *chin boss*, a phenomenon were the chin is wrinkled and pushed closer to the lips.[103]

---

[95] Ekman and Friesen 2003, pp. 116–117
[96] Ekman 2007, p. 97
[97] Ekman and Friesen 2003, pp. 117–119
[98] Ekman 2007, 97 f.
[99] Ekman and Friesen 2003, pp. 117–119
[100] Ekman 2007, p. 102
[101] Ekman and Friesen 2003, p. 119
[102] *ibid.*, pp. 119–121
[103] Ekman 2007, p. 98

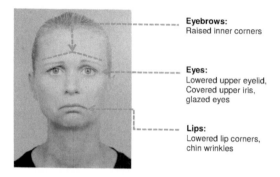

Eyebrows:
Raised inner corners

Eyes:
Lowered upper eyelid,
Covered upper iris,
glazed eyes

Lips:
Lowered lip corners,
chin wrinkles

Figure 7: Signs of Sadness (Eilert 2013, p. 77)

4.2.2.6 *Anger*

Anger belongs to the negative emotions and is the most dangerous emotion, because anger can lead to physical or psychological violence as we try to harm the object or person that caused our anger. Another dangerous characteristic of anger is that anger itself calls forth anger so that anger that you point at someone else can cause this person to become angry at you.[104]

Sternberg and Campos found in their research from 1990 that one of the most effective ways of provoking anger (in infants) is physical interference, e.g. by holding their arms so they cannot move them.[105] This example shows one of the most frequent triggers for anger in children and adults. If something or someone interferes with our intent on doing something, we become angry towards this person or object. Other emotional triggers for anger include responses to physical or psychological violence that is directed towards us, rejection by people we care about, injustice or even the frustration about an object.[106]

By considering the intensity and the circumstances, different types of anger can be differentiated. In terms of intensity, anger can reach from slight annoyance about something to rage, accompanied by physical violence. Furthermore, the type of anger can vary between indignation, sulking, exasperation, revenge or resentment.[107]

Anger comes with several bodily changes. Depending on the intensity of the emotion, the blood pressure increases, face reddening occurs, veins become more apparent through the higher blood pressure, and

---

[104] *Ibid.*, pp. 112–114
[105] Sternberg and Campos 1990, 247 ff.
[106] Eilert 2013, p. 70
[107] Ekman 2007, p. 112

there might be a movement towards the offending person to encourage the emotional message.[108] In order to perceive anger in facial expressions, besides the other mentioned signs, we have to focus on three major parts of the human face, as the most important signs of anger are displayed through the eyelids, the eyebrows and the mouth.

The **Anger Brow** occurs when both eyebrows are lowered slightly and the inner corners of the brows are drawn together, so that they appear to be lower than normal or point downward. In general, the lowering of the brows causes the appearance of vertical wrinkles between the brows, while horizontal wrinkles on the forehead do not appear, unless they are permanent wrinkles of the face.[109] Normally, if a person experiences anger, the anger brow is accompanied by the anger mouth and eyes. Standing alone with an otherwise neutral expression of the face, anger brows are no proof of anger and can therefore be a sign for controlled anger, slight annoyance, concentration or feeling perplexed.[110]

The **Anger Eyes** can occur in two different ways, open and narrow, and are mostly defined by tensed eyelids. Raising and tensing the lower lid causes the eyes to become narrower but still more open than the second type of anger eyes. The narrow anger eyes can only appear in combination with the anger brow, as the lowered brow pushes against the upper eyelid and is therefore responsible for the narrowing of the upper part of the eye. Similar to the alone standing anger brow, anger eyes alone are no proof for anger and even the combination in form of the narrow anger eyes leaves space for reasonable doubt, if the person is slightly angry, concentrated or any of the mentioned above.[111]

The **Anger Mouth** is the third sign that is associated with the expression of anger in human faces. Similar to the anger brows, the anger mouth can appear in two variations, with open and narrowed lips. The open anger mouth occurs often during conversation when the anger is expressed through verbal communication like shouting. In contrast, pressing the lips together and forming the narrowed anger mouth occurs when people try to restrain their anger and hold back themselves from shouting.[112] Even though the anger mouth is also ambiguous, the narrowing and tensing of the lips is often a reliable and early sign of beginning or highly controlled anger.[113]

---

[108] Ekman and Friesen 2003, p. 80

[109] ibid., p. 82

[110] Ekman 2007, p. 139

[111] Ekman and Friesen 2003, p. 83

[112] ibid., pp. 83–88

[113] Eilert 2013, p. 70

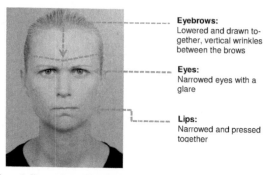

Eyebrows:
Lowered and drawn to-
gether, vertical wrinkles
between the brows

Eyes:
Narrowed eyes with a
glare

Lips:
Narrowed and pressed
together

Figure 8: Signs of Anger (Eilert 2013, p. 71)

As the previous paragraphs clearly illustrate, each single sign of anger is ambiguous and thus, Paul Ekman notes that *"The facial signals of an-ger are ambiguous unless there is some registration of the anger in all three facial areas."* [114] Nevertheless, partial facial expression in combina-tion with other signs such as veins, a reddened face or a step forward can be proof of anger.[115]

Now that we have learned to recognize and interpret basic emotions, we go one step further, focusing on facial expressions that are even hard-er to recognize and need a higher amount of training and attention in or-der to perceive them.

4.2.3 Subtle Expressions

The previous chapters about the signs of facial expressions already intro-duced that not all areas of the face are necessarily involved in the facial expression of an emotion. This mainly results from the attempt of a person to control the facial expression out of several reasons, such as social norms. Even though, macro expressions are considered to be voluntary movements that can be controlled, a study by Hurley and Frank has shown that the attempt to suppress them only results in a reduction of nonverbal signs but never in a complete suppression.[116]

This type of facial expression is called subtle facial expression and re-fers to a partial macro expression. Besides the attempt of suppressing a macro expression, subtle expression can also occur when an emotion is just beginning or when the intensity of the emotion is comparatively low.[117]

---

[114] Ekman and Friesen 2003, p. 88
[115] Eilert 2013, p. 71
[116] Hurley and Frank 2011, pp. 119–131
[117] Eilert 2013, p. 58

The challenge with subtle expressions is that the signs are ambiguous and cannot be assigned to a specific emotion without considering other factors. For example, a subtle expression, such as the anger brow, can be a sign for anger but also for concentration. Hence, a negotiator should always be aware of the different meanings that subtle expressions can have and evaluate the expression with respect to the circumstances of the negotiation.

4.2.4 Micro Expressions

Emotions are not always expressed through "long-lasting" macro and subtle expressions which increases the difficulty of interpreting emotions in others. These shorter versions of facial expressions are called micro expressions and due to the shorter duration of display, they are extremely difficult to recognize.[118] For this reason, the last chapters discussed the individual characteristics of each emotion to increase the consciousness for emotional expressions that is needed to detect micro expressions faster and more reliable.

The challenge with facial macro expressions is that people are able to control them and use faked facial expressions to hide true emotions and deceive other people. Therefore, the only way to detect concealed emotions is to focus on micro expressions.

A micro expression is defined as a short version of a macro expression that reveals the true emotional state of a person who tries to conceal his emotion. These expressions are also displayed on the face through the movement of muscles, especially in regions around lips, eyebrows, mouth and nose.[119] According to Paul Ekman, a person is able to fake facial expressions but before the faked macro expression appears on the face, a micro expression will leak beforehand and reveal the true emotional state.[120] This leakage occurs because micro expressions are triggered directly through the limbic system that evaluates external stimuli 500ms faster than the cerebral cortex that controls the macro expressions.[121] Due to this lead in time, the micro expression will flash before the controlled macro expression appears on the face.

Ekman distinguishes between two major motives of why micro expressions occur. First, when people try to hide their own emotions from themselves (unconscious concealment) and second, when they intentionally conceal their emotion from others (deliberate concealment).[122]

The main characteristics of a micro expression are the involuntary leakage and the short duration.[123] Therefore, the most important differ-

---

[118] Hurley *et al.* 2014, p. 700

[119] Nermend and Łatuszyńska 2016, p. 137

[120] Ekman and Friesen 1969, 88 f.

[121] Eilert 2013, p. 55

[122] Ekman and Friesen 1969, 88 f.

[123] Yan *et al.* 2013, p. 226

ence between macro expressions and micro expressions is the on- and offset time as well as the duration of the expression. Statistical research showed that micro expressions only last between 170ms for the lower limit and 500ms for the upper limit,[124] compared to a macro expression that lasts from 0.5s to 4s.[125]

The actual importance of the ability to detect micro expressions became clear when Ekman and Frank were able to identify deception through micro expressions with an accuracy of 80% during an experiment. Thereafter, they claimed that every well-trained person can reach a similar accuracy of detecting deception based on emotional micro expressions.[126]

But the field of application for micro expressions is even more diverse and therefore applicable in nearly every situation. For example, the TSA in the United States introduced the "Screening Passengers by Observation Techniques" to identify potential threats by analyzing facial expressions of passengers. Furthermore, micro expression detection is used in clinical psychology or in the analysis of political speeches to uncover emotions and detect deception.[127] Other applications of micro expression recognition include lie detection, crime investigations or the analysis of customer responses to marketing campaigns.[128]

The above mentioned application examples lead to the conclusion that micro expressions can also be helpful and advantageous for negotiations, as deception and lies are often involved in negotiations. Therefore, the next chapter will focus on the nature of lies and the influence of emotions and facial expressions on the ability to detect deceit.

---

[124] *ibid.*, p. 229

[125] Scherer and Ekman 2014, p. 332

[126] Frank and Ekman 1997, p. 1433

[127] Yan *et al.* 2013, p. 218

[128] Wezowski and Wezowski 2012 **qtd. in** Nermend and Łatuszyńska 2016, p. 138

5 Understanding Emotions in the Context of a Negotiation

5.1 Deception and Lies[129]

The previous chapter introduced how every emotion becomes visible through different facial expressions. Those facial expressions are especially helpful when it comes to lies and deception. Negotiations often involve deception and lies and so it is not surprising what an article about lies in business already revealed in 1981:*"Perhaps the most famous lie of all is: 'That's my final offer.' Such language is not only accepted in business world, it's expected. ... During collective bargaining, for example, no one is expected to put all his cards on the table at the outset."* [130] This shows that lies are an accepted and expected part of negotiations so the purpose of this chapter is not only to bring attention to this fact but to analyze how emotions and facial expressions can help a negotiator to advance in lie detection in order to improve his bargaining position.

First of all, it is necessary to define the nature of a lie, and to distinguish between the major types of lies. Lying and being untruthful is often used interchangeably but is it actually a lie when you do not even know that the information you are providing for someone else is not true?

A leading expert in lie detection, Paul Ekman, defines a liar as a person who intentionally misleads others. While a person who is not telling the truth cannot be called a liar because he does not even know he is not telling the truth, a real liar chooses between the lie and the truth and knows the difference between both. In addition, a lie can only be considered to be a lie if the misleading person gave no prior notification about the intention to lie and was not explicitly asked by the other person to do so.[131] For example, attending a magic show is such a special case, where misleading is not considered a lie because it is the nature of magicians to mislead the audience.

Deceit can be distinguished in terms of the type of the lie and also with respect to the intention or content of the lie.[132] The two major types of lies that are discussed below are concealment and falsification.

Concealment is the easiest form of lying as it does not involve the necessity of telling the untruth and making up a story to cover the truth. Instead, the misleading person is telling the truth while leaving out specific

---

[129] Lie and deceit is used interchangeably within this paper
[130] Horowitz 1981, p. 81
[131] Ekman 2009, pp. 26–27
[132] Eilert 2013, p. 183

details. While concealment is often preferred because it is easier than falsifying, it is also preferred because it seems to be less morally reprehensible due to its passive character. Furthermore, concealment lies are also easier to cover in case they are discovered because of the variety of possible excuses, such as the intent of revealing it at a later point.[133]

Falsification is the second way of lying that requires much more attention and preparation than concealment. Falsifying helps the liar to cover the evidence of the truth that he wants to conceal by masking the true emotion and adding, leaving out or changing details when telling the story.[134]

Besides the different types of lies, there are also different intentions or contents of a lie. When someone is lying, he either lies about emotions or information. If a poker player is dealt a good hand, he will likely try to conceal his happiness in order to keep the information from his opponents. Or, if you negotiate about a price and you are already satisfied by the offer but want to get a bigger discount, you would conceal your happiness as well. Besides the emotional part, people also lie about information, such as the "Last Price" mentioned above, as well as plans and thoughts.[135]

The challenge with identifying lies is that no one is able to read someone else's mind and therefore we need to rely on other indicators. The best chance of identifying deceit is to focus on something that is hard to control and will most likely leak while someone is lying, the microexpressions of emotions. The following chapters therefore deal with common masking techniques and the primary reasons of why lies fail or in other words, they show how to spot indicators of deceit through leaking emotions.

5.1.1 Masking Deceit

In general, every emotion can occur during the process of lying but some are more often intertwined with deceit than others, just as some masking techniques are more often used than others. Before discussing the three meta-emotions any further, we will focus on how most people mask their deceit.

The most common mask that is used by liars is the smile. The first reason why liars choose the smile to mask emotions and lies is that smiling is a universal standard of greeting and most negotiations or conversations frequently require smiling as a sign of politeness.[136] But even more important for the choice is the simplicity of a smile. As mentioned before (see chapter 4.2.2.3 about happiness and enjoyment), a smile is mainly expressed in the lower face which is easier to control voluntarily than the upper parts, such as the eyebrows. An untrained negotiator will likely miss

---

[133] Ekman 2009, pp. 29–30
[134] Eilert 2013, pp. 183–184
[135] ibid.
[136] Ekman 2009, p. 35

the subtle differences between a fake smile and a Duchenne smile which explains the popularity of using the smile to mask other emotions. Nevertheless, there are other indicators such as too quick or too slow on- and offset times or even completely false timing of the smile that can identify it as a mask.[137] On the other hand, negative emotions are rather difficult to falsify due to their appearances in the upper face that are harder to make for most people. Thus, a deceit that requires negative emotions is more likely to be discovered.[138]

5.1.2 The Three Meta-Emotions of a Lie

Even though a false smile might already reveal a lie, it often requires much more attention and focus to identify possible clues. Important to note is that all of the described clues of leakage are nothing more than "hotspots". These hotspots are points during a conversation that might indicate a lie but require further investigation, such as questioning or evaluation of the circumstances, before making false accusations.[139] The most common emotional hotspots for deceit are the fear of detection apprehension, the guilt about lying and the delight in having duped another person.[140]

5.1.2.1 *Detection Apprehension*

The emotion that most often accompanies a lie is fear, or more precisely the fear of getting caught.[141] Paul Ekman refers to this phenomenon as "detection apprehension". When this fear appears in a milder form it can actually be advantageous for the misleading person as it helps to avoid mistakes and keeping the focus. Nevertheless, in more intense forms, which happen to be more probable, different determinants influence the intensity of the fear felt and increase the likelihood of getting caught.[142]

The first influencing determinant is the reputation of the liar as well as the reputation of the person who is the target of the deceit. If the target is known to be easy to deceive, the fear of getting caught in the liar will be less intense but on the other hand, if the target is known to be a good lie catcher, the fear intensity will increase accordingly and might reveal information the liar wanted to conceal.[143]

Secondly, the character of the deceiver plays a key role in the intensity of the felt detection apprehension. Some people have a harder time than

---

[137] *ibid.*, p. 36

[138] *ibid.*

[139] Eilert 2013, p. 182

[140] Ekman 2009, pp. 49–79

[141] Eilert 2013, p. 186

[142] Ekman 2009, p. 49

[143] *ibid.*, pp. 49–52

others when lying.[144] People who are confident in deceiving others and do not feel intense detection apprehension share characteristic with a psychopathic personality. But this is only a similarity and no classification as natural liars who are highly skilled in deceit do have a conscience that is absent in psychopathic personalities. This ability is especially helpful in certain professions such as acting, practicing law, selling and negotiating.[145]

The last determinants for the intensity of detection apprehension are the stakes that are involved in the deceit. The higher the stakes, the higher is the detection apprehension rising in the liar. The stakes can either be defined as a reward, e.g. bonuses, or punishment, such as losing the job or the trust of a loved person.[146] For example, a negotiator will experience a more intense fear when he is negotiating a deal with a high commission or if a successful deal increases his chances of getting a promotion.

Due to the fear, micro-expressions of emotions, such as described in the chapter about fear, can leak and function as a hotspot for detecting a lie. A good negotiator will always be aware of the three previously described determinants and will be able to increase the fear of his opponent in order to provoke micro expressions. Important to note is that an excellent negotiator will only increase the fear in the one who is not telling the truth, while a trustworthy person will relax. This can be accomplished by further questioning the other person on details, establishing a reputation as a good lie catcher or by bringing the consequences of a liar to the liar's attention.[147]

The only challenge that remains with pressuring someone is that the fear of detection apprehension and the fear of an innocent person do not differ in terms of expression and thus, signs of fear are ambiguous.[148] Therefore other factors, such as the environment, have to be considered in order to ensure that the perceived fear is caused by a lie and not by other circumstances.

5.1.2.2 Deception Guilt

The second emotion that often appears when someone is trying to deceive another person is guilt. When someone is feeling guilty for his deceit, it is important to distinguish that deception guilt is not concerned with the content of the lie but with the guilt felt about deceiving the other person.[149] Similar to fear, also deception guilt can vary in intensity, depending on different determinants.

---

[144] ibid., p. 54
[145] ibid., pp. 57–58
[146] ibid., pp. 59–64
[147] Eilert 2013, pp. 186–187
[148] Ekman 2009, pp. 52–53
[149] Eilert 2013, p. 187

Most important, the interpersonal relationship between the liar and the target is influencing the intensity of deception guilt. The better the relationship between the two parties, the more guilt will be felt towards the target. Thus, every comment on the good relationship or the expression of trust during the conversation will increase the chance that the liar will feel more intense guilt and leak it through facial expressions or body language.[150] Besides the relationship there are other determinants that increase deception guilt; the target derives no advantage from being deceived, the liar and the target share social values, the liar does not see any personal advantage through his deceit (altruistic lies) or the liar is not experienced in lying to others.[151]

On the other hand, some factors might decrease the intensity. Most often the guilt decreases, when the deceit is authorized or the liar thinks that the deceit is legitimate. For example, a poker player with a good hand might feel fear of getting caught but guilt is rather rare as deceiving the other players is part of the game and there is no reason to feel guilty about misleading them.[152]

Guilt itself has not been described as part of the basic emotions due to the fact that it is not universal. Nevertheless, guilt is an emotion that belongs to the emotion family of sadness and shares distinctive features with sadness.[153] Shame is another emotion from the sadness family that is closely related to guilt and often comes along with a lie. The main difference between guilt and shame is that guilt does not require any judgements of an audience, while shame requires the disapproval by others.[154]

Both, guilt and shame, are expressed through similar expressions that can also be observed in the expression of sadness. The facial expressions in the three main areas of the face are exactly the same so the signs are ambiguous unless other expressions can be observed. Besides the expression of sadness in the face, guilt and shame are also expressed through other body movements that distinguish guilt and shame from sadness. Most often, people who feel guilt or shame avoid eye contact, touch or cover their face with their hands or lower their head and look downwards (mainly to the left). Furthermore, the voice can reveal guilt and shame because guilty or ashamed people usually decrease their volume and speed of voice and talk less in general.[155]

Sometimes, when people do not feel guilty about lying, there is another emotion that can appear, even though it is quite rare: duping delight.

---

[150] ibid.
[151] Ekman 2009, pp. 75–76
[152] Eilert 2013, p. 188
[153] ibid., p. 86
[154] Ekman 2009, p. 65
[155] Eilert 2013, pp. 83–87

5.1.2.3 *Duping Delight*

Duping delight is basically the opposite of deception guilt. Rather than feeling guilty about misleading someone, the act of deceiving is a delightful experience for the deceiver. The deceit itself may be seen as an accomplishment for the liar and he might feel excitement, pleasure or even contempt towards the target.[156]
The intensity of duping delight is usually the greatest when the target is known to be a good lie catcher and thus it is difficult to deceive him or if the lie itself is a challenge in terms of the story that has to be fabricated or the details that have to be concealed. Last but not least, it is increased when an audience is observing the lie and admires the ability of the liar to deceive someone.[157]
In contrast guilt that is sometimes expressed to emphasize that the liar regrets his action of deceiving,[158] most people try to conceal the "morally reprehensible" duping delight. For this reason, they are showing signs of suppression as they try to cover a smile by pressing together the lips and drawing down the corners of the lips to prevent them from rising.[159]

Being aware of the three meta-emotions of a lie is an advantage that negotiators can use to increase the effectiveness of negotiations. By uncovering deceit, negotiators can precisely focus on revealing the concealed information. This information about interests or contractual details can be advantageous in focusing on win-win agreements, as the basis of integrative negotiations is the communication of information. Furthermore, this awareness about the interdependence of emotion and deceit can help a negotiator to protect himself from being deceived and closing disadvantageous deals.

---

[156] Ekman 2009, pp. 76–77
[157] *ibid.*, p. 79
[158] Eilert 2013, pp. 83–87
[159] *ibid.*, p. 189

5.2 Different Personalities Require Different Negotiation Approaches

Every single negotiation is different and so are the involved negotiators. Psychological, personal and situational factors determine the strategies and tactics that are used by a negotiator and influence his style of negotiating. The differences in negotiation styles are based on the differences in personality and there are as many personalities as there are people.

Personality traits are defined as measurable tendencies of a person to feel, act and think in a certain way. Due to these characteristics, they are especially suited for the prediction of human behavior.[160] To simplify the classification of personality, researchers identified clear definitions for five personality traits that summarize the majority of traits and enable us to easily classify other people according to these identified traits.

In the following these personality traits will be introduced as well as an additional personality trait that has a major influence on negotiations.

5.2.1 The Big Five Personality Traits

As the previous chapter already introduced, people have different personalities and thus, some people are more prone to be impacted by emotions than others and the same emotions may result from different triggers. In the following, the concept of the "Big Five" personality traits will be introduced and evaluated on the grounds of how negotiation strategies need to be adapted accordingly.

Personalities are complex and therefore not easy to define and describe in a unified way. One approach that found wide acceptance across personality psychologists is the Five-Factor Model of Personality that focuses on five key personality categories that summarize most individual personality traits.[161] The "Big Five" are defined as openness to experience, extroversion, conscientiousness, agreeableness, and neuroticism.[162]

Openness to experience is the personality trait that focusses on creativity and the openness towards innovation and change. Low scoring people in openness (O-) are often very experienced and have a broad knowledge in a specific area of interest. They are seeking for efficiency and often refuse change as they prefer traditional procedures. Besides, they are considered to be data and fact-oriented which makes it harder to convince or influence them through emotional strategies. On the other hand, a high scoring person (O+) is considered to be an innovator. Creativity and change is not only accepted and wanted but an innovator also gets bored very fast and seeks for new innovations. This makes him a

---

[160] Geiger 2016, p. 230
[161] Lewicki *et al.* 2015, p. 464
[162] Goldberg 1990, p. 1217

good customer for innovative products while low scoring people that pre-fer tradition can be loyal long-term customers to a company once they acquired its product. Furthermore, high scoring people pay less attention to details than low scoring people and therefore they do not insist on small matters during negotiations rather than focusing on the overall contract, which can save time and effort.[163]

Extroversion is the personality trait that is most often associated with negotiators and salesman. It is the contrast between an outgoing (E+) and an introverted or reserved personality (E-), e.g. Muhammad Ali was a highly extroverted person while Bill Gates has a more reserved personali-ty. Introverted persons often prefer tasks and jobs that do not require too much social interaction. They rather work alone and try to avoid face-to-face communication which can lead to the impression that introverted persons are cold and secluded. In contrast, extroverted persons enjoy social interactions and want to take centre stage. They are talkative, en-thusiastic and action-oriented but sometimes, especially in combination with an introverted person, they often lack in listening skills. This tendency of dominating conversations can lead to frustration in the other negotiator as he feels misunderstood. Furthermore, this dominant behavior could be interpreted as aggressive, inconsiderate or superficial by others and trig-ger anger, contempt or frustration in the other party. Nevertheless, their enthusiasm and ability to show and use positive emotions to influence and persuade others is considered to be a major skill of an excelling negotia-tor/salesman.[164]

The third of the Big Five personality traits is **conscientiousness**. High-ly conscientious people (C+) are disciplined, reliable, organized and fo-cused persons. They often work in management positions or positions with high independence, where organizational skills and determination are required to lead a team and succeed. In contrast, low scoring persons (C-) have a more flexible working style and prefer spontaneous procedures which enable them to work on different projects simultaneously. When negotiating with highly conscientious people, it is very important to plan ahead and do not show up unexpected or unprepared.[165]

Besides extraversion, **agreeableness** is the second personality trait that plays a special role in a negotiators personality. It reflects people's intentions towards social harmony. People with a challenging personality (A-) are most often skeptical towards others. They are defined by charac-teristics such as independence, resilience or competitive and aggressive behavior in order to protect their interests. Even though these characteris-tics are positive traits for negotiators, challenging persons can seem to be egocentric, hostile and aggressive in the eyes of others. In contradiction to the challenging personality, people who are more adaptive (A+) are char-

---

[163] Howard and Howard 2002, pp. 61–72
[164] ibid., pp. 49–60
[165] ibid., pp. 85–96

acterized through helpfulness, team spirit, tolerance and acceptance. They rather give up on their own positions and let others win than insisting on their own opinions. This accommodating nature makes them prone to emotional influence as they tend to become emotionally touched easily. This also leads to the assumption that adapting persons are easy to fool, dependent, and servile.[166] A combination of both (A=), adaption and provocation, is the personality trait that the Harvard Negotiation Concept proposes for principled negotiators in order to find win-win situations, due to the fact that neither hard nor soft negotiating leads to mutually beneficial agreements.

The last personality trait is **neuroticism**, also referred to as emotional stability. Due to the focus of this paper on the impact of emotions on effective negotiations, this trait is especially important. Neuroticism measures the ability of coping with stressful situations and also the tendency of experiencing negative emotions such as anger, guilt or fear. In the chapter about deception and lies, it already became clear that negative emotions are the source of leakage for deception. People with an emotionally stable personality (N-) are less likely to suffer from deception guilt or detection apprehension. Furthermore, it is more difficult to pressure them as they have a very calm personality and a high awareness of how to cope with stress. They might make the impression of being indifferent as they often suppress emotions and proceed in an analytical and reasonable manner. On the other hand, reactive people (N+) with a high score in neuroticism often react impulsively and experience negative emotions much faster and more intense.[167] Their proneness for emotions is much higher than for emotionally stable people and therefore it is harder for them to resist pressure and maintain deceits. Besides, their emotional instability increases the likelihood of experiencing anger, the most dangerous emotion, or any other negative emotions. Therefore it is even more important to pay attention to rising negative emotions in order to apply diminishing strategies as early as possible.

5.2.2 Machiavellianism

Even though the Big Five are already covering a majority of traits, there is another personality trait that should be considered in terms of negotiations. Machiavellianism has been repeatedly investigated in negotiation research due to its major impact on negotiation behavior.

People with a high degree of Machiavellianism (M+) are only focusing on their own interests and objectives and are not afraid of applying manipulation techniques to achieve their objectives.[168] High Machs tend to be skeptical towards others objectives, behave selfish and often unpleasant towards their negotiation partners. Besides, they are more tolerate in

---

[166] *ibid.*, pp. 73–84
[167] *ibid.*, pp. 37–48
[168] Brooks and Rose 2004, p. 125

terms of ethically questionable negotiation approaches and they are also more inclined to the use of deception, e.g. making false promises or misrepresenting interests.[169] This mindset also enables high Machs to use deception with less signs of leakage than low Machs would show. The lack of awareness for ethics and moral lowers the intensity and likelihood of suffering from deception guilt. Due to the fact that high Machs tolerate the use of deception and deceive others themselves, they feel less guilty about lying. This makes high Machs extremely dangerous as they are not seeking for win-win negotiations rather than self-interest based outcomes.

As a result, Machiavellianism often leads to distributive negotiations as high Machs are only interested in their own objectives. Their behavior may intimidate the opposing negotiator into changing his strategy which may lead to worse negotiation results and harmed relationships.[170] Insisting on personal objectives and "winning" is valued higher than customer satisfaction or long-term relationships.

When signs of high Machiavellianism appear throughout a negotiation, special attention should be paid to the behavior of the negotiator in order to identify deception techniques as early as possible and to take countermeasures.

5.2.3 The Influence of Personality on the Negotiation Strategy

The previous chapters illustrated that a personality consists of different traits that are more or less distinctive. In other words, every person has one or more trait(s) that are dominant and have the highest influence on their behavior. Nevertheless, the other traits are also part of their personality but they are less dominant and can be arranged hierarchically based on their importance.[171]

In order to use the knowledge about someone else's personality for personal advantage throughout a negotiation, it is most important to identify dominant, compatible and incompatible personality traits (traits that you do or do not share with your negotiation partner).[172] The individual differences and similarities amongst the personality of the negotiators mainly impact the strategies that can be used in order to emotionally influence the other negotiator.

The challenge with identifying personality traits in general and also their dominance is that you cannot ask a negotiation partner to complete a personality test prior to the negotiation. Thus, it is even more important to know your own personality traits as good as possible as it raises the awareness for matching and differing traits in the negotiation partner. Furthermore, the awareness and knowledge about facial expressions of emotions gives you the advantage of understanding how others feel, how in-

---

[169] Lewicki *et al.* 2015, pp. 461–462
[170] *ibid.*, p. 462
[171] Howard and Howard 2002, p. 128
[172] *ibid.*, pp. 128–129

tense the feelings are and where their origin is. By collecting this information throughout the conversation, it is possible to sketch a profile of your negotiation partner that enables you to adapt your strategy to the personality of the negotiation partner.

For the personal negotiation strategy this means that some negotiators have better prerequisites than others and their knowledge and emotional intelligence enables them to adapt their behavior in a way that focuses on increasing positive emotions and diminish negative ones. Excellent salespersons or negotiators for example often share the same personality traits and therefore it might be easier for them to use influencing strategies as their personalities are matching. Nevertheless, also negotiators with a different personality profile than the opposing negotiator can be successful. The only difference is that they often have to adapt more often and use strategies that do not match their natural preferences.[173]

In order to simplify the process of deciding on specific negotiation strategies, a model has been developed as part of this paper. This Model can be used by negotiators who already identified dominant traits in their negotiation partners and need to decide on specific negotiation strategies.

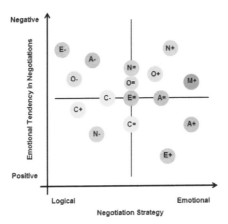

Figure 9: Decision Matrix for the Selection of Negotiation Strategies and Tactics [174]

The proposed decision matrix classifies the different personality traits according to their characteristics into two dimensions. First, the emotional

---

[173] *ibid.*, pp. 135–136
[174] Derived model based on the characteristics of the Big Five and Machiavellianism

tendency of a negotiator that evaluates if positive or negative emotions are more likely to occur during the negotiation and second, the dimension of the negotiation strategy which classifies the different personality traits according to their proneness for logical or emotional negotiation strategies and tactics.

Based on this classification and the dominant personality traits of the other person, the negotiator can identify if a logical or emotional negotiation strategy will be more successful. Furthermore, the decision matrix indicates if the other person is more prone for negative or positive emotions during a negotiation. For example, a person with a dominant A+ personality is more prone for emotional persuasion techniques and tends to experience positive emotions more often during a negotiation than negative emotions. Therefore, less attention has to be paid toward the signs of negative emotions than it would be necessary with an A- personality.

Now that we have identified the influence of personalities on the negotiation strategy, we are going to focus on a set of specific influencing techniques. Based on personality types, variations of these techniques can be used to diminish negative and stimulate positive emotions. As for this paper, the focus will be on emotional strategies and tactics.

6 Strategic Use of Emotions in Negotiations

6.1 The Difference Between Positive and Negative Emotions

In general, emotions can be distinguished into three categories; positive, negative and neutral emotions that, such as surprise, lead to either positive or negative emotions. During a negotiation there are always several emotions that come and go over time but sometimes it is necessary to get actively involved and diminish negative emotions or stimulate positive emotions.

The reason for getting actively involved is that emotions do have a major impact on the efficiency and effectiveness of the negotiation. As mentioned in the beginning, emotions influence the human behavior, as they motivate us, help us to communicate and enable us to make decisions. The difference between positive and negative emotions in general is that positive emotions are beneficial to negotiations while negative emotions often jeopardize the negotiation.

One of the first empirical studies on the influence of emotions on integrative negotiations from 1986 by Carnevale and Isen showed that positive affect decreased the competitive behavior and had a positive influence on the effectiveness of negotiations.[175] According to this and several follow up studies by Allred[176], Anderson and Thompson[177], and Carnevale[178] that replicated the findings, negotiators with a positive emotional mindset can achieve integrative outcomes more easily than negatively minded negotiators. Besides, positive emotions or affects have a positive impact on the tendency to expand the relationship.[179] In addition, positively minded negotiators enjoy more trust, increase the overall level of trust between each other[180] and, in certain circumstances, positively minded negotiators can expect more concessions than negotiators who transfer negative emotions. Nevertheless, expressed positive emotions can also backfire when they are recognized as false praise in order to manipulate the other side.[181]

Similarly, negative emotions can also have both, negative and positive effects during a negotiation. Some negotiators express anger to gain an

---

[175] Carnevale and Isen 1986, p. 7
[176] Allred *et al.* 1997, pp. 175-187
[177] Anderson and Thompson 2004, p. 130
[178] Carnevale 2008, pp. 51–63
[179] Geiger 2016, p. 248
[180] Anderson and Thompson 2004, p. 130
[181] Baron 1990 **qtd. in** Druckman and Olekalns 2008, p. 2

advantage, e.g. by expressing anger about a contractual detail, hoping to trigger fear in others who respond with concessions to sooth the situation.[182] Nevertheless, negative emotions most often lead to worse negotiations. Negative emotions, such as anger, disappointment or distrust, decrease the ability to think clearly and creatively towards an integrative solution. Furthermore, they can also trigger negative emotions in others and lead to more competitive and even inappropriate behavior.[183] Concluded, negative emotions should be used with caution or at least, they should be limited to one negotiation.

In the following, specific strategies and tactics are introduced that can be used by negotiators to influence positive and negative emotions for more effective negotiation experiences. Due to the fact that diminishing negative emotions is more important and often encourages positive emotions such as trust, satisfaction or excitement, the focus will be on strategies to temper anger, distrust, and other negative emotions.

6.2 The Classification of Emotional Negotiation Strategies and Tactics

In the following chapters, six different strategies and tactics will be introduced that negotiators can use during negotiations. For this purpose, a model has been developed that classifies the negotiations according to two dimensions.

First, the strategy or tactic in a negotiation is influenced by the overall "Emotional State". This emotional state refers to the type of emotion that appears. In this context, the model differentiates between positive and negative emotions, due to the fact that both require different approaches.

Second, the intensity of the emotion is a major factor of influence. The emotional intensity is represented by the dimension "Emotional Temperature". For example, a low temperature of anger would be slight annoyance while a high emotional temperature is represented by fury.

The main purpose of the developed classification model is to indicate the latest point where a strategy definitely has to be considered or used. While mirroring can be used for all emotional states and temperatures, changing the players only has to be considered for strong negative emotions. Other strategies such as tactical empathy can be used similarly to mirroring but should definitely be considered as soon as emotions are shifting from positive to negative and the emotional temperature is rising.

---

[182] Fisher and Shapiro 2005, p. 152
[183] ibid., pp. 146–147

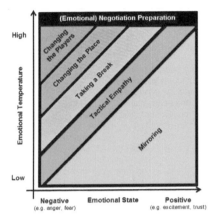

Figure 10: Classification Model for Emotional Negotiation Strategies and Tactics

The strategies illustrated in the model are only examples for strategies that can be used for emotional negotiations. Thus, the model does not include all potential strategies and can be expanded with other strategies according to the classification criteria.

6.2.1 Strategies to Diminish Negative and Stimulate Positive Emotions

Based on the introduced classification model, the exemplary strategies and tactics will be further described in the next chapters in order to demonstrate their influence on emotions and negotiations.

6.2.1.1 Emotional Negotiation Preparation

People become more cooperative when experiencing positive emotions. Besides being positively influenced by their own emotions, the emotions of the negotiation partner also have a high impact on their emotions. Therefore it is important to prepare emotionally before entering a negotiation, as a positive emotional mindset positively influences you and your negotiation counterpart.

One emotion that most often occurs before negotiations is anxiety. Especially inexperienced negotiators tend to be anxious prior to a negotiation. Studies by Schweitzer and Brooks in 2011 revealed that anxious negotiators make lower first offers, respond rashly to new moves and show the tendency to exit negotiations earlier. In addition, the agreements of negotiators who experienced and showed anxiety were, from the financial view, 12% less attractive.[184] These less attractive agreements that result from anxiety can also lead to disappointment and dissatisfaction about the own performance after the negotiation. Besides, contempt can be felt towards the other party if deceit was involved. In order to prevent anxiety, disappointment and contempt in yourself and the other negotiator, different techniques can be used.

First of all, anxiety is a reaction to threatening stimuli,[185] where the outcomes are not predictable. Thus, preparing for the negotiation and training your negotiation skills decreases anxiousness, as the training and preparation gives you confidence in your abilities. Furthermore, training and preparation will change the view on negotiation and increase the level of comfort. Besides reducing the anxiety, this preparation also proactively increases positive emotions such as excitement. Thus, the negotiator can look forward to negotiations and new opportunities with excitement instead of anxiety. As a result, calmness will increase and anxiety will be tempered which leads to more effective negotiations.[186]

6.2.1.2 Mirroring

Trained negotiators know that they have to be prepared for possible surprises; great negotiators do not only know that surprises will come, they also use their skills to reveal the surprises that exist. They do not accept articulated statements but question them and thus remain emotionally open to changing situations.[187]

The key of revealing information that others would just wait for is building trust. Great negotiators know that people only share information when there is a certain level of trust and a positive atmosphere. To establish this trusting and harmonic atmosphere, experts use a technique that most of us only use unintentionally, mirroring. Mirroring, or reflective listening, is a way of implying similarities that facilitate interpersonal bonding between the negotiation parties and encourage them to reveal new information without even noticing that you asked for it.[188]

Mirroring is relatively simple but effective in its application, even though, in the beginning, this technique might be uncomfortable for most people. Starting with a simple smile to signal empathy and a calm tone of voice, the negotiator copies the behavior of the other person and repeats the last three words (or the most important words) of what the other person just said before pausing until the other side reacts.[189] The intention of a mirror usually is to transfer the message that he is in need of further understand-

---

[184] Wood Brooks 2015, pp. 56–58
[185] ibid., p. 56
[186] ibid., pp. 58–59
[187] Voss 2016, pp. 18–19
[188] ibid., p. 31
[189] ibid., p. 24

ing, while signaling concern and respect for the argumentation. In general, this will cause the other person to rephrase what they have just said. This is the important part as the rephrased message will never be the same and most often new information will be revealed.[190]

The art of mirroring requires the use of emotional intelligence. People are more likely to share information with people they trust and where a rapport has been established. Therefore, showing interest and active listening through mirroring is essential in order to create an emotionally positive atmosphere and build rapport, which encourages trust and the willingness to share information with others.

6.2.1.3 *Showing Tactical Empathy*

In negotiations it often happens that frustration and anger result from the feeling that the other side is not listening. Even when the technique of mirroring is used by a negotiator, there might still be misunderstandings left. A tactic to show that you are actively listening and appreciating the other side's opinion is to use tactical empathy.

Empathy is the ability to recognize the other side's perspective but also the vocalized response to that recognition. Beyond this simple empathy is tactical empathy. Tactical empathy further requires that the negotiator is able to recognize and understand the involved emotions and the mindset of the other person and also being able to identify what is behind those emotions. Once the emotional barriers are identified, potential solutions can be developed in order to find an agreement.[191]

The tactic that is used to express empathy is called labeling. Labeling is the process of translating recognized emotions into words which are repeated in a calm and respectful way back to the other person. When phrasing the response to an emotion through labeling, it is important to phrase them as neutral questions or statements by avoiding to use "I", e.g. "It seems like you are disappointed" rather than "I think this is disappointing you". Staying neutral prevents a defensive attitude and encourages the other person to be responsive and explain their feelings because they realize that the interest is in them and not yourself. Furthermore, labeling is a de-escalating tactic due to the fact that labeling fears or anger helps others to acknowledge their emotions instead of letting them out.[192]

Showing empathy and labeling negativity helps to interrupt emotional processes in the amygdala. A labeled emotion loses its power because as soon as the negativity is spoken in words, it seems to be less important and frightening. Thus, it instantly becomes easier to support positive emotions once the negative ones have been diminished.[193]

---

[190] *ibid.*, pp. 29–30
[191] *ibid.*, p. 33
[192] *ibid.*, pp. 35–36
[193] *ibid.*, p. 38

The key to success when using tactical empathy is to understand and find merit in what the other person is saying before communicating it. Plainly labeling a fact will not result in de-escalation as it might seem like hypocrisy rather than appreciation. Only true understanding of the other person's feelings and views will be recognized as empathy and helps to diminish negative emotions and encourage a cooperative and motivational atmosphere.[194]

6.2.1.4 *Taking a Break*

Taking a break is one of the easiest techniques that can be used during a negotiation. As soon as the emotional temperature within the environment is rising, asking for a short break can cause a significant decrease of emotional intensity and prevent emotional outbursts.[195] For example, some people, such as introverted persons, do not enjoy long meetings and sometimes they are even afraid and feel a high amount of discomfort when joining long negotiations with many people. On the other hand, when two extroverted persons are negotiating and both lack in listening skills as they try to dominate the negotiation, misunderstandings and lacking progress may call forth anger. In these situations, taking a short break can give all participants the time to soothe down. Besides, the time can be used to reevaluate the emotional behavior and temperature of all participants in order to identify the emotional triggers and develop new strategies to prevent further negative emotions.

Another advantage of taking a break is that it gives the involved negotiators the time to recapitulate the recent progress and planning further steps. Especially when there is a negotiation deadlock and there has not been any progress for a longer period, frustration can appear within all participants as there is no common ground. Taking a break at this stage of the negotiation can help all negotiators to free their minds and think about strategic ways to move forward.[196]

6.2.1.5 *Changing the Players or the Place*

Sometimes, when the emotional temperature is rising and negative emotions are taking over the negotiation, taking a break might not be a sufficient solution for diminishing negative emotions. Emotions are, other than moods, always directed towards a specific object, stimulus or person.[197] Hence, a negotiation might be in jeopardy because the negative emotions are linked to the negotiators themselves or the place of the negotiation and always reoccur due to the emotional memory.

---

[194] Fisher and Shapiro 2005, p. 51
[195] *ibid.*, p. 153
[196] *ibid.*
[197] Zimbardo *et al.* 2008, p. 454

In this case, the only solution might be to change the players or the place for a while in order to prevent the negative emotions that are directed towards them. For example, selecting neutral locations such as restaurants or coffee shops for the next meeting can diminish the influence of emotional triggers such as colleagues or superiors and emphasize a more positive emotional starting position for further negotiations.[198]

The presented strategies only represent a fraction of the strategies that can be used by negotiators to actively use emotions in order to increase the efficiency of the negotiation. Nevertheless, the discussed selection should raise the awareness of how emotions can improve the negotiation efficiency.

---

[198] Fisher and Shapiro 2005, pp. 153–154

7 Conclusion

The thesis revealed that emotions influence negotiations in certain ways, such as communication, motivation and decision making. Essential to influencing these three areas of negotiating is the awareness of emotions and their characteristics as well as an overall understanding of emotions which can be summarized as emotional intelligence.

Especially the recognition of emotions through facial expressions is an important skill that enables negotiators to identify emotions. While recognition of emotion might be simple for macro expressions, the differentiation between macro, -micro and subtle expressions showed that emotion recognition requires a high amount of knowledge, awareness and attention, due to the fact that most signs of emotions have a short and subtle appearance.

Nevertheless, facial emotion recognition enables negotiators to identify not only emotions but also deception techniques and to reveal information and interests of the other party. This information about interests is the basis of integrative negotiations that enables negotiators to reach mutually beneficial agreements.

Furthermore, the ability to recognize emotions through facial expressions enables negotiators to identify the individual personality traits of other negotiators. As every negotiator has a different personality, the applicable negotiation strategies have to be adapted accordingly. By classifying personalities through emotion recognition, negotiators are enabled to decide whether or not the other person is prone for emotional or logical negotiation strategies. In addition, the understanding of the interdependence between emotions and personality can be used by negotiators to decide on specific persuasion techniques that match the other person's natural preferences.

Through the application of emotional negotiation strategies and tactics, negotiators are able to positively influence the negotiation environment. This most often leads to more attractive win-win agreements, due to the fact that a positive emotional negotiation environment encourages the trust between the negotiators which is essential in order to negotiate successfully.

In conclusion, the difference between a good negotiator and an excellent negotiator is the ability to perceive and understand emotions and use the right emotion (or strategy) authentically at the right time to positively influence the negotiation.

8 References

Allred *et al.* 1997
    Allred, K. G., C. P. Raia, J. S. Mallozi, and F. Matsui.
"The influence of anger and compassion on negotiation
performance.", *Organizational Behavior and Human Decision,* 1997.

Anderson and Thompson 2004
    Anderson, Cameron and Leigh L. Thompson. "Affect from
the top down. How powerful individuals' positive affect
shapes negotiations." *Organizational Behavior and Human Decision Processes* 95:2 (2004), pp. 125–139.

Baron 1990
    Baron, Robert A. "Environmentally Induced Positive Af-
fect. Its Impact on Self-Efficacy, Task Performance, Negotiation, and Conflict." *Journal of Applied Social Psychology* 20:5 (1990), pp. 368–384.

Baron 2013
    Baron, Rober A. "Conflict in Organizations." In Kevin R.
Murphy and Frank E. Saal, eds., *Psychology in Organizations. Integrating Science and Practice, Applied Psychology Series.* Hoboken: Taylor and Francis, 2013.

BBC News Online 2016
    BBC News Online. *Bayer confirms $66bn Monsanto
takeover,* 2016. Available at
http://www.bbc.com/news/business-37361556, 20 Sep-
tember 2016.

Brandstätter *et al.* 2009
    Brandstätter, Veronika, Jürgen H. Otto, and Jürgen
Bengel, eds. *Handbuch der allgemeinen Psychologie -
Motivation und Emotion,* / published by J. Bengel … ;
Bd. 11 of *Handbuch der Psychologie.* Göttingen:
Hogrefe, 2009.

Brooks and Rose 2004
    Brooks, Bradley W. and Randall L. Rose. "A contextual
model of negotiation orientation." *Industrial Marketing
Management* 33:2 (2004), pp. 125–133.

Carnevale 2008
Carnevale, Peter J. "Positive affect and decision frame in negotiation." *Group Decision and Negotiation* 17:1 (2008), pp. 51–63.

Carnevale and Isen 1986
Carnevale, Peter J.D and Alice M. Isen. "The influence of positive affect and visual access on the discovery of integrative solutions in bilateral negotiation." *Organizational Behavior and Human Decision Processes* 37:1 (1986), pp. 1–13.

Damasio 1995
Damasio, Antonio R. *Descartes' Error. Emotion, reason and the human brain.* New York: Avon Books, 1995.

Darwin 1872
Darwin, Charles. *The Expression of the Emotions in Man and Animals.*

Druckman and Olekalns 2008
Druckman, Daniel and Mara Olekalns. "Emotions in negotiation." *Group Decision and Negotiation* 17:1 (2008), pp. 1–11.

Duchenne and Cuthbertson 2006
Duchenne, Guillaume Benjamin and R. Andrew Cuthbertson. *The mechanism of human facial expression, Studies in emotion and social interaction.* Cambridge i.a.: Cambridge Univ. Press, 2006.

Eilert 2013
Eilert, Dirk. *Mimikresonanz. Gefühle sehen, Menschen verstehen, Reihe Fachbuch Kommunikation & Mimik.* Paderborn: Junfermann, 2013.

Ekman 1994
Ekman, Paul, ed. *The nature of emotion. Fundamental questions, Series in affective science.* New York NY i.a.: Oxford Univ. Press, 1994.

Ekman 2007
Ekman, Paul. *Emotions revealed. Recognizing faces and feelings to improve communication and emotional life.* New York: Owl Books, 2007.

Ekman 2009

Ekman, Paul. *Telling lies. Clues to deceit in the marketplace, politics, and marriage.* New York: W.W. Norton, 2009.

Ekman and Friesen 1969

Ekman, Paul and Wallace V. Friesen. "Nonverbal Leakage And Clues To Deception.", *Psychiatry Journal For The Study of Interpersonal Processes,* 1969.

Ekman and Friesen 2003

Ekman, Paul and Wallace V. Friesen. *Unmasking the face. A guide to recognizing emotions from facial expressions.* Cambridge,MA: Malor Books, 2003.

Fehr and Russell 1984

Fehr, Beverley and James A. Russell. "Concept of emotion viewed from a prototype perspective." *Journal of Experimental Psychology: General* 113:3 (1984), pp. 464–486.

Fisher and Shapiro 2005

Fisher, Roger and Daniel Shapiro. *Beyond reason. Using emotions as you negotiate.* New York NY: Penguin Books, 2005.

Fisher and Ury 2011

Fisher, Roger and William Ury. *Getting to yes. Negotiating agreement without giving in.* New York NY i.a.: Penguin Books, 2011.

Frank and Ekman 1997

Frank, Mark G. and Paul Ekman. "The Ability to Detect Deceit Generalizes Across Different Types of High-Stake Lies.", *Journal of Personality and Social Psychology,* 1997.

Gardner 2011

Gardner, Howard. *Frames of Mind. The Theory of Multiple Intelligences.* New York, NY: Basic Books, 2011.

Gary Player n.d.

Gary Player, n.d. Available at http://bit.ly/2gXAyre, 20 December 2016.

Geiger 2016

> Geiger, Ingmar. "Negotiation Management." In Michael Kleinaltenkamp, Wulff Plinke and Ingmar Geiger, eds., *Business Project Management and Marketing, Springer Texts in Business and Economics*. Berlin, Heidelberg: Springer Berlin Heidelberg, 2016.

Goldberg 1990

> Goldberg, Lewis R. "An Alternative "Description of Personality": The Big-Five Factor Structure.", *Journal of Personality and Social Psychology,* 1990.

Häusel 2014a

> Häusel, Hans-Georg, ed. *Neuromarketing. Erkenntnisse der Hirnforschung für Markenführung, Werbung und Verkauf, Haufe Fachbuch.* Munich: Haufe Lexware Verlag, 2014.

Häusel 2014b

> Häusel, Hans-Georg. *Think Limbic! Inkl. Arbeitshilfen online ; Die Macht des Unbewussten nutzen für Management und Verkauf,* v.10109 of *Haufe Fachbuch.* s.l.: Haufe Verlag, 2014.

Horowitz 1981

> Horowitz, Bruce. "When Should an Executive Lie?" *Industry Week* (1981).

Howard and Howard 2002

> Howard, Pierce J. and Jane Mitchell Howard. *Führen mit dem Big-Five-Persönlichkeitsmodell. Das Instrument für optimale Zusammenarbeit.* Frankfurt/Main: Campus-Verl., 2002.

HOWTOMEDIA n.d.

> HOWTOMEDIA, INC. *http://www.innerbody.com,* n.d. Available at http://www.innerbody.com.

Hurley *et al.* 2014

> Hurley, Carolyn M., Ashley E. Anker, Mark G. Frank, David Matsumoto, and Hyisung C. Hwang. "Background factors predicting accuracy and improvement in micro expression recognition.", 2014.

Hurley and Frank 2011

> Hurley, Carolyn M. and Mark G. Frank. "Executing Facial Control During Deception Situations." *Journal of Nonverbal Behavior* 35:2 (2011), pp. 119–131.

Levenson 1994
Levenson, Robert W. "Human Emotion: A Functional View." In Paul Ekman, ed., *The nature of emotion. Fundamental questions, Series in affective science.* New York NY i.a.: Oxford Univ. Press, 1994.

Lewicki *et al.* 2015
Lewicki, Roy J., David M. Saunders, and Bruce Barry. *Negotiation.* New York, NY: McGraw-Hill Education, 2015.

McGinn 2011
McGinn, Colin. *The meaning of disgust.* New York: Oxford University Press, 2011.

Nermend and Łatuszyńska 2016
Nermend, Kesra and Małgorzata Łatuszyńska. *Selected issues in experiementes economics // Selected Issues in Experimental Economics.* Cham: Springer International Publishing, 2016.

2014a. *Orbicularis Oculi,* 2014. Available at http://bit.ly/2hEm28V, 11 December 2016.

Paul Ekman 1970
Paul Ekman. "Universal Facial Expressions of Emotions." *California Mental Health Research Digest* (1970), pp. 151–158.

Rahim 2001
Rahim, M. Afzalur. *Managing Conflict in Organizations.* Westport, Conn: Quorum Books, 2001.

Rhudy and Meagher 2000
Rhudy, Jamie L. and Mary W. Meagher. "Fear and anxiety. Divergent effects on human pain thresholds." *Pain* 84:1 (2000), pp. 65–75.

Richard Lazarus 1994
Richard Lazarus. "Meaning and Emotional Development." In Paul Ekman, ed., *The nature of emotion. Fundamental questions, Series in affective science.* New York NY i.a.: Oxford Univ. Press, 1994.

Roth 2009
Roth, Gerhard. *Fühlen, Denken, Handeln. Wie das Gehirn unser Verhalten steuert,* vol. 1678 of *Suhrkamp-Taschenbuch Wissenschaft.* Frankfurt am Main: Suhrkamp, 2009.

Salovey and Mayer 1990
Salovey, P. and J.D. Mayer. "Emotional intelligence. Imagination, Cognition, and Personality.", 1990.

Scherer *et al.* 1990a
Scherer, Klaus Rainer, Carl F. Graumann, and Niels Birbaumer, eds. *Psychologie der Emotion*, ; V. 3 of *Enzyklopädie der Psychologie Theorie und Forschung Motivation und Emotion*. Göttingen: Hogrefe Verl. für Psychologie, 1990.

Scherer *et al.* 1990b
Scherer, Klaus Rainer, Carl F. Graumann, and Niels Birbaumer, eds. *Psychologie der Emotion*, ; V. 3 of *Enzyklopädie der Psychologie Theorie und Forschung Motivation und Emotion*. Göttingen: Hogrefe Verl. für Psychologie, 1990.

Scherer and Ekman 2014
Scherer, Klaus R. and Paul Ekman. *Approaches To Emotion*. Hoboken: Taylor and Francis, 2014.

Schiewer 2014
Schiewer, Gesine Lenore. *Studienbuch Emotionsforschung. Theorien, Anwendungsfelder, Perspektiven*. Darmstadt: WBG (Wiss. Buchges.), 2014.

Schmitz-Atzert *et al.* 2014
Schmitz-Atzert, Lothar, Martin Peper, and Gerhard Stemmler. *Emotionspsychologie. Ein Lehrbuch, Standards Psychologie*. s.l.: Kohlhammer Verlag, 2014.

Sternberg 2000
Sternberg, Robert J. *Handbook of intelligence*. Cambridge i.a.: Cambridge Univ. Press, 2000.

Sternberg and Campos 1990
Sternberg, C. R. and J. J. Campos. "The development of anger expressions in infancy." In Nancy L. Stein, ed., *Psychological and biological approaches to emotion*, C. R. Sternberg and J. J. Campos. Hillsdale NJ i.a.: Erlbaum, 1990.

Ury 2007
Ury, William. *Getting past no. Negotiating in difficult situations*. New York, NY: Bantam Books, 2007.

Voss 2016
   Voss, Christopher. *Never split the difference. Negotiating as if your life depended on it.* New York: HarperBusiness an imprint of HarperCollins Publishers, 2016.
Walton and MacKersie 1991
   Walton, Richard E. and Robert B. MacKersie. *A behavioral theory of labor negotiations. An analysis of a social interaction system.* Ithaca, N.Y: ILR Press, 1991.
Wezowski and Wezowski 2012
   Wezowski, Kasia and Patryk Wezowski. *The Micro Expressions Book for Business: How to read facial expressions for more effective negotiations, sales and recruitment:* New Vision, 2012.
Wood Brooks 2015
   Wood Brooks, Alison. "Emotion and the Art of Negotiation." *December 2015 issue (pp.56–64) of Harvard Business Review.* (2015), pp. 56–64.
Yan *et al.* 2013
   Yan, Wen-Jing, Qi Wu, Jing Liang, Yu-Hsin Chen, and Xiaolan Fu. *How Fast are the Leaked Facial Expressions. The Duration of Micro-Expressions,* vol. 37, 2013.
Zimbardo *et al.* 2008
   Zimbardo, Philip G., Richard J. Gerrig, and Ralf Graf. *Psychologie, PS Psychologie.* München: Pearson Studium, 2008.
2014b. *Zygomaticus Major Muscle.* Available at http://bit.ly/2hfeT1E, 11 December 2016.

Appendix

Appendix A1: The Zygomaticus Major
Appendix A2: The Orbicularis Oculi

Appendix A1: The Zygomaticus Major

The zygomaticus major muscle is one of the facial expression muscles involved in a smile. Its main function is to aid in articulation of the mouth, nose and cheeks. In a smile, the zygomaticus major raises the corners of the mouth and enables a person to smile.[199] Due to the fact that the zygomaticus major can be contracted voluntarily, it is involved in a Duchenne smile as well as a social smile.[200]

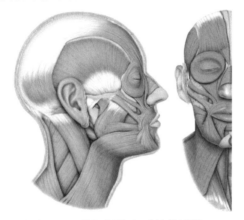

Figure 11: The Zygomaticus Major (2014b, http://bit.ly/2hfeT1E)

---

[199] HOWTOMEDIA n.d., http://bit.ly/2hElbF4
[200] Ekman 2007, pp. 204–207

Appendix A2: The Orbicularis Oculi

The orbicularis oculi is a circular shaped muscle band that surrounds the eye. Its major function is to cause the eye to close or blink but it also compresses the nearby tear gland to aid the flow of tears to moisten the surface of the eye.[201]

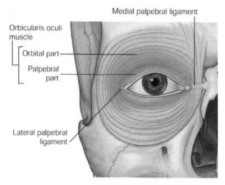

Figure 12: The Orbicularis Oculi (2014a, http://bit.ly/2hoYPZg)

Besides the mentioned functions, the orbicularis oculi muscle is also involved in the Duchenne smile. The contraction of the muscle causes the appearance of wrinkles or crow's feet at the outer corner of the eye. The involvement of the orbicularis oculi is an unambiguous sign for a true smile as the contraction cannot be controlled voluntarily and therefore is absent in a social smile.[202]

---

[201] HOWTOMEDIA n.d., http://bit.ly/2hoYPZg
[202] Ekman 2007, pp. 204–207

YOUR KNOWLEDGE HAS VALUE

- We will publish your bachelor's and master's thesis, essays and papers

- Your own eBook and book - sold worldwide in all relevant shops

- Earn money with each sale

Upload your text at www.GRIN.com
and publish for free